THE *Worship* MANUAL

Leading God's People Under an Open Heaven

by

SARENINA Y. BONNER

Watersprings
PUBLISHING

THE WORSHIP MANUAL
Published by Watersprings Publishing, a division of
Watersprings Media House, LLC.
P.O. Box 1284
Olive Branch, MS 38654

Library of Congress Control Number: 2019936111

ISBN 13: 978-1-948877-12-1

CONTENTS

FOREWORD

I met Sarenina Bonner in the fall of 2015 and while working with her almost every day, I have developed a warm friendship as well as a working relationship with her. I have found her to be a passionate worshiper and someone who loves to encourage others in their worship relationship with the Lord. I have seen her take on more and more worship leadership responsibility at her local church and as she has encountered challenges, Sarenina readily seeks the counsel of others. She loves to pray and seek the face of the Lord for wisdom, discernment and any other grace gift that will help her to become a better worship leader.

The Worship Manual, by Sarenina Bonner, covers many aspects of worship, from describing what worship is, how it is depicted throughout the Bible, how the worshiper is affected by true worship, and the effect of true worship on the church.

Sarenina beautifully describes the four different types of worshipers that are present in any worship gathering. She writes about the critic, the performer, the "religious" worshiper and the worshiper who is pure in heart. At the end of each of these descriptions, Sarenina challenges the reader to reveal their hearts by answering penetrating questions.

Miss Bonner shares her own personal journey from being a worshiper to becoming a worship leader. She clearly outlines the stages of her growth and her own learning throughout this experience. She shows us that God is interested not only in our gift, but in our character and how that can be developed. She also shows the pitfalls that we must avoid, such as pride, independence and unconfessed sin.

This book is instructive and informative. It includes instruction for the worshiper, the worship leader, the team leader, as well as the pastor in his interaction with the music and worship leaders. Every human being on earth worships something. Sarenina points the readers to those things that help them all, no matter what their role, to become true worshipers.

There are possibly many topics that Sarenina has covered in this manual that you may not have thought of. Please do not ignore them. If something is new to you, discuss it with others, or present it before the Lord in prayer. There were things that Mary the mother of Jesus heard from others that she did not understand. The shepherds delivered a message to her, Simeon spoke to her, Anna the prophetess spoke words to her. She did not discard these things; the scriptures tell us, *"She pondered these things in her heart"*. This is my encouragement to you; ponder things in your heart that you may not readily understand or that you have not known or experienced. May this worship manual be a blessing to you in whatever area you serve, or whatever position that you have within the Body of Christ.

John Johnson
Worship Leadership Division Head, Visible Music College

ACKNOWLEDGEMENTS

All gratitude and glory goes to God! He's a good Father who's perfect in every way and in timing. I want to acknowledge Watersprings Publishing and Athena C. Shack who operated in excellence and with execution. I thank you from the bottom of my heart for every email, text, word of encouragement, loving correction, and hug. This divine connection has truly enriched my life. Words cannot express how thankful I am that God used you as a midwife to help birth this vision. I love you!

I acknowledge and give honor to my mother, Twyla Pigues, who unknowingly walked the path that God had for her in order that I would begin the journey of finding my purpose. Due to you allowing me to cultivate my God given talents, I stumbled upon my gifts. Thank you for your support and unconditional love. I want to thank my amazing mentors Clayborn and Lakeshia Momon. Your amazing influence, godly counsel, correction, and guidance have truly helped set me free from fear and shame. I am grateful for the place you hold in my life.

To my *Purpose Fulfilled* sisters, thank you for being a sounding board. Your words of encouragement reminded me that I can do all things with Christ who gives me perfect strength. For the times I doubted, you were there. To my dear friend, Lady Carol Davis, who immediately looked at my transcript and said, "This is a book and you need to write it. What are you waiting for!" Thank you for your direct push and your direct love. I appreciate you. To the vessels Lameko Taylor and Cory Smith, that God used very directly to confirm this book God had given me, thank you for your obedience. I pray God will give you a return on your obedience.

Most of all to the spiritual leadership God has placed me under, Apostle Tony and Pastor Felecia Wade, I honor you. I want to say thank you and I love you both. Your leadership, the training, the hard conversations and the many meetings were used to rebuild the woman I now am. I cannot repay you for the mark you have made on my life, but I will forever honor you and the position you hold naturally and spiritually. Thank you, Mom and Dad, for seeing what God wrote in my books and helping me to taste and see. And to every atmosphere I have ever encountered, thank you for the resistance that led to the making of a worship leader.

INTRODUCTION

"I'm called to be a worship leader!" If I've heard it once, I've heard it a thousand times. Well how do you know? Who told you that? When people come to me and say this, I laugh. I immediately think to myself, "Wow! I hope you're ready!" Prayerfully, God has shown you your destiny and if it involves leading people into a deeper place of worship while bringing glory to Jesus, that's amazing. I'll challenge you and say that you are NOT called to be a worship leader. You were CHOSEN to be His worship leader! You are called to be a worshiper. A worshiper of God the Father, Christ the Holy Son, and the precious Holy Spirit. See, that's the thing about it. Many Christians identify with the stage and the lights, the amazing band, and the most appropriate, befitting song, but many do not understand the innermost workings of worship. What it is, and what it is not. We are "anointed" but we lack revelation! We lack knowledge. We lack wisdom. We lack depth. We even lack roots. In this book, you will get an in-depth look at worship. Not just for leading worship but for living worship.

The Holy Spirit instructed me months ago to write a book about worship and then to teach people how to do it. My immediate thought was, "How can I do that? I am not seasoned enough." He replied, "Write about what I've shown you up until this point. What I give you, you share and when I add to you, you will share more." Isn't that amazing! See... it is not about age. It is not my tenure in worship leading, or in worship ministry that qualifies me. It is the revelation from the Holy Spirit, and the posture of my heart that has allowed me to receive the outpouring from those wiser and more established than me. He qualifies me!

If you look for me wholeheartedly, you will find me.
Jeremiah 29:13 NLT

When you search wholeheartedly, God can do something so unique and beautiful in you, and then turn around and say give it away. What I have learned in worship ministry is that I know nothing at all. I only have what Jesus has given me, and what I need to know for the assignments given up until this point in my life. If I am willing to remain teachable and pliable, He will then give me more, and it will be what is needed for the next assignment. God is just amazing like that. Jehovah Jireh continues to be a provider for what is needed before you even think to request it.

What makes a good manual is credibility. So, I have some other sources that provide amazing teaching and training that I have included in this book. I encourage you to purchase those books as well. My prayer for you is that through you reading this, you learn what I have lived. I pray you grow leaps and bounds in your walk with Jesus. My prayer for myself is that lives will be changed from this manual. I can only trust that because of my obedience to complete this task, you will give Him your YES! This manual is designed for you to examine your heart and assess how your worship is received from the true and living God. Because the Holy Spirit didn't want to isolate anyone, there is something in here for everyone. If you feel that this only applies to someone on a stage leading, then I can't wait for you to read!

Here are a few ground rules when reading:

1. Be open minded.
2. Take notes and highlight, please :)
3. Evaluate yourself.
4. Everything does not apply to you, so eat the meat and toss the bones.
5. While this book will go into quite a bit of detail, please know that every question you have will not be answered. Seek the Holy Spirit. He knows all!
6. Grow your ministry of worship. Application!
7. Be the Change you wish to see.
8. Draw Closer to Christ.

I am grateful you desire to grow in your knowledge of worship, I planted the seed, and God gives the increase. Revealed knowledge comes from the King of Kings and is only revelation once it has been applied!

In obedience,

Sarenina Y. Bonner

11

1

The Worship

Worship is not defined in the Bible, it is described! The Bible does not provide a literal definition of what worship is, however, it is full of examples of what worship was, is, and is to come. The Bible communicates what should be, and what occurred that God considered to be worship unto Him. Worship according to Webster is reverence offered a divine being or supernatural power. Extravagant respect or admiration for, or devotion to, an object of esteem. Worship is simply an organic (sincere) expression, display, and response of adoration and reverence to the Lord. In order to reverence and adore something or someone you have to know them, AND you have to acknowledge who or what they are.

> *From here on, worshiping the Father will not be a matter of the right place but with the right heart. For God is a Spirit, and he longs to have sincere worshipers who worship and adore him in the realm of the Spirit and in truth.*
> *John 4: 23-24 TPT (The Passion Translation)*

Too often we quote, declare and decree John 4:23-24 to emphasize it to be the standard, or the mark in which we should strive to meet. It has been coined as what worship is. The scripture has been clichéd and the revelation of "in spirit and in truth" has been void. We've adopted this in our church language and if you ask people what it means, they could not tell you. What I am saying is, if you do not have a revelation of what it means, then how can you be so sure you're truly executing it? In the passage, Jesus is speaking to the Samaritan woman and He is answering her question from the previous verse. She asks which way (location), is the right way to worship. He then tells her and everyone that worship is not about the place, it's about the heart. Not the way but the why. He is looking for sincerity, and worshipers that will worship the totality of who He is.

Worship is also described as sincerity and acknowledging the Trinity. Those who worship Him must worship Him… who is Him? The Trinity. The Triune God. The Godhead. Three in One. The Father, Son and the Holy Spirit. Comprehending worship is acknowledging the Trinity. God is our Creator and Father. We can't get to Him unless we gain access through the Son, and then the Holy Spirit is the person who leads us and gives us insight. Jesus is the truth and the Holy Spirit is the spirit of Jesus that is now here on the earth for us and with us. Although in John, the Holy Spirit had not been introduced until we see Him in Acts 2, the Holy Spirit is God and was with God in the beginning. Trinitarian worship is the fullness of response. There are a number of ministries that do not possess a balance of the Trinity in their prayer language, song selection and/or their sermons.

To not acknowledge the Trinity is to not acknowledge the totality of God. You cannot tell me you know Him if you do not recognize all of Him. You are missing out on true worship.

Jesus told him, "I am the way, the truth, and the life. No one can come to the Father except through me.
John 14:6 NLT

In the beginning [before all-time] was the Word (Christ), and the Word was with God, and the Word was God Himself. He was [continually existing] in the beginning [co-eternally] with God. All things were made and came into existence through Him; and without Him not even one thing was made that has come into being.
John 1:1-3 AMP

God has brought all things into existence and they exist for Him. Worship begins in the beginning! We see this concept of God working, speaking, and then creation comes into existence. It is important to understand that creation has been given a command to exist, to function, and then creation in return obeys the command. They simply worship.

Everything on earth will worship you; they will sing your praises, shouting your name in glorious songs.
Psalm 66:4 NLT

> And then I heard every creature in heaven and on earth and under the
> earth and in the sea. They sang: "Blessing and honor and glory and power
> belong to the one sitting on the throne and the Lamb forever and ever."
> *Revelation 5:13 NLT*

Noel Due says, "Worship, then does not begin with human beings as though they alone worship, or as if they are the initiators of worship. Worship begins with God. By virtue of His very being as God, and by virtue of His act of creation, God is the initiator of worship. It begins with God and it was very evident in the celestial and terrestrial creation before human beings were brought into existence. This means that when God created our first parents, they came into a worship-filled creation. By implication their existence was also to be taken up in worship."

We see in Genesis where Adam dwelled in Eden. Not only did he live there, but he fellowshipped there. He communed there. Eden is described as the glory of God housed. You may rebuttal and say, "Adam was not singing the top 10, and didn't have an anointed musician, or an instrumental piano worship soaking playlist." No, he did not. What he had was revelation! He lived in the Glory. He was aware of Glory. The Bible tells us that God gave a command and he responded. He worshiped! Worship is first described as response. Adam worshiped God with obedience and faithfulness. As a result of the response, Adam gained relationship and God was there with him. So fast forward to when Eve comes on the scene. Adam fell due to responding to the lie or the darkness. He responded to the serpent, meaning when he partook of the fruit, he then worshiped the enemy. Why? Because he responded. As long as he responded to God he was in relationship with God, he was alive spiritually and he thrived naturally, physically, and emotionally. But when he responded to the enemy, he lost relationship, and he no longer worshiped in spirit and in truth.

When you respond to God's truth and His command you prosper. You show your allegiance by what you worship or respond to. We were created to worship God. We were made for His pleasure.

The Importance of the Old Testament

Many only view the Old Testament as an archive and have little knowledge of why the Old Testament is so important. We cannot understand the New Testament without the Old Testament. It lays the framework for the foundations of faith and is a foretelling of what's to come. In the Old Testament we begin to understand God's ways and His heart toward His children, sin, law and obedience. The Old Testament lays a foundation of worship. Worship was according to the revelation of God that was realized at that point. Before Samaria and before Acts, the people of God had aspects of God. I think it was divinely designed for God to reveal who He was and provide us with many facets of Himself before the revealed knowledge of Jesus Christ His son and the Holy Spirit were introduced. There is clear instruction on what is deemed acceptable and what is deemed unacceptable. It introduces the character of God, and it provides instruction for our lives through stories of the ones who came before us. Since God is the same yesterday, today and forevermore then His words in the old covenant hold true today.

As it relates to worship, I love the Old Testament. It is the first and greatest commandment in both the old and new covenant. In the scriptures we are taken to the beginning of creation, then we move forward to Cain and Abel and we begin to see a concept of worship unfolding. Noel Due states in Created for Worship, the principle of "Canaanite Worship" (to coin a phrase) is one of self-justification. For those who worship according to the line of Cain, a worship is a means to an end- the end being one's own blessing, the means being on one's own terms. Then we move on to Noah. We see that God recognized Noah as a righteous man and blameless among the people. As God gives Noah instruction for His plan to wipe or cleanse the earth, Noah obeyed. Worship is living an upright life and obedience.

> *So, Noah did everything exactly as God had commanded him.*
> *Genesis 6:22 NLT*

Questions:
1. What is God commanding you to do?
2. Have you done it JUST as He commanded?

The theme of obedience and faithfulness goes throughout the Old Testament. Abraham worshiped God with obedience. When he was instructed to kill Isaac, he rose early to obey. He did not hesitate to follow the command, God found delight in Abraham. He also did not bow to false Gods. It is important to consider people like Moses, Miriam, Aaron, David, Asaph, King Jehoshaphat and others who are considered leaders of worship and praise. Reading the Old Testament and taking the principles and practices from their lives will show you how God used people to do His will, and how they responded in obedience, worship, praise, and surrender.

The Power of the Psalms in Worship

Psalms is a beautiful poetic work of art. It gives a very vivid and realistic view on praise, worship, war, distress, repentance, anger, joy and love. If you ever need a model of how to pray, or to see how transparent you can get with the Lord, look at the Psalms. They work well for worship because our lives are comprised like many of the Psalms. We have trials, shortcomings, enemies, and sin that invade our lives and hinder us in relationship with the Lord. But knowing that God's faithfulness, and His mercy is available to us even when we do not want to receive it, is an amazing way to tell the Gospel story in worship. I also appreciate the concept of lament in the Psalms. The acknowledgement of real issues, real thoughts, and real sin, but then the confession, repentance, and praise that follows just gives a true visual of the Christian walk. It provides another element to the template of pure worship. The template of worship is praise and thanksgiving and you add in vulnerability and truth. Thank the Psalmist for providing such elaborate praise Psalms that give reverence and adoration to the Lord. The Psalmist

18

had a heart of thanksgiving, and a heart of gratefulness. Praise exuded from his being. Praise was ever on his lips, so should it be for us as worshipers. We should look to the word of God and more importantly, the Psalms to show us how to form our words when it comes to exhortation to the Holy One.

WORSHIP: WHAT IT IS VS. WHAT WE MAKE IT

> **Worship**: reverence (respect) and adoration (deep love)

I find it interesting when people describe and define worship. They say, "worship is what we are to do." They reference the songs they enjoy listening to, or the prominent gospel artist that they listen to while they pray. I've heard so much as, "It's honor to God. It's what we give back to God." I would say that it is that, and so much more. Our own very description of worship can limit His mightiness and power. Looking up the definition of worship, Webster clearly defines worship as a verb to honor or reverence as a divine being or supernatural power and to regard with great or extravagant respect, honor, or devotion. Most would agree, because they have been taught that it's what we do.

The body of Christ has become so divided in the way we gather before the presence of the Lord. We have taken the Bible and instead of abiding by the whole book, we break it up into sections. Believers have compartmentalized Christianity because in doing that we can remain in our conditions and not require our lives to begin to truly reflect Christ's ways. Some denominations believe in music and some don't. Some are so religious and have rules like not clapping or lifting their hands, no dancing, communion every Sunday, communion once a month, celebrate, Pentecost is over with, freedom for the Holy Spirit to move, or speaking in tongues is wrong and an old teaching. We have so many rules and restrictions that we forget about God. He is not this far away ghostly being that gives us goosebumps or has this long waiting list before He can get to us. He is Immanuel. God with us. He desires to be with us and to be worshiped. It brings Him pleasure.

I would categorize worship as a verb and noun. Worship is what we do and who we are. We were created by the Almighty God for the purpose of worship. Worship is designed to give God glory. It is an outward expression of reverence and honor to the Creator. That is my definition. Meanwhile we, the body of Christ, and non-believers alike, have turned worship into a mockery and a ritual of mundane expression and routine. We have robbed God of glorious worship because we have embraced the selfish fleshy nature more than the adaptation of the new creation we've become in Christ. It speaks volumes when the unbeliever doesn't even desire relationship with Christ, or salvation, because we have taken playing church to another level by spitting on such a sacred display of love and relationship such as worship. Let's dive into this more!

Outward vs. Inward Worship

> *And so, the Lord says, "These people say they are mine. They honor me with their lips, but their hearts are far from me. And their worship of me is nothing but man-made rules by rote.*
> *Isaiah 29:13 NLT*

There is so much to glean from the verse above. Jesus was not impressed with the religious or systematic act of worship and expressed it through Isaiah. I have learned that you cannot worship without the Originator teaching you. The Holy Spirit knows what is appropriate and acceptable. He will teach you how to worship.

When you bow, kneel, cry out, praise and shout, that's an outward expression of praise and worship. The body of Christ puts so much pressure on having an outward expression. They gauge connection by the display of outward expression during a worship setting but have no understanding that inward expression is what the Lord searches for. The outward expression of worship should be a direct reflection of your inward posture/expression. Anyone can lift their hands and lay prostrate but when the Holy Spirit asks you to sow a seed to a sister in Christ, or to give a brother in Christ a word of knowledge, are you obedient? If you shouted in church but did not participate in tithes and offering, then you still have missed what is acceptable to God. He views worship as obedience to His command and His law. Examine your inward worship expression because God does. Remember the best way to understand the nature of God is to

21

1) look at the example of His Son Jesus; 2) read His word. Just like Samuel thought Eliab was anointed (chosen) because of his appearance, because of his outward expression but God sees and examines the heart (inner expression). If your heart isn't yielded, then you're not yielded. If your heart isn't devoted to worshipping the true and living God, then what is it worshipping. It could be worshipping the idea of your future. We could worship our very purpose. God doesn't want us to be so focused on what He said concerning us that we lose sight of who said it. We all subconsciously do it.

> But the Lord said to Samuel, "Don't judge by his appearance or height, for I have rejected him. The Lord doesn't see things the way you see them. People judge by outward appearance, but the Lord looks at the heart.
> 1 Samuel 16:7 NLT

WHERE DO WE WORSHIP?

We worship at His footstool. We worship at His holy mountain. We worship the Lord at the splendor of holiness. We worship God acceptably with reverence and awe.

> And so the Lord says, "These people say they are mine. They honor me with their lips, but their hearts are far from me. And their worship of me is nothing but man-made rules learned by rote.
> Isaiah 29:13 NLT

Worship is not about the right place but the right heart. So, we can physically worship anywhere. Everywhere. Jesus addressed this concept of having specific places to worship God. When the Samaritan woman inquired on where they will go worship Jesus told her that there will come a time where the mountain and the temple will no longer matter. The legalities do not matter. We no longer need a priest to go before us and prepare the way. The High Priest Jesus did that when He died on the cross and rose on the third day. See the veil was torn and now our worship is no longer predicated on such rules. Believers, you are no longer tied to just Wednesday and Sunday mornings. You can be in your car, in your home, in the park, on your job, washing dishes, in your bedroom or in the corporate gathering of believers. As long as your worship is located in your heart, any place and any posture is appropriate and acceptable. Your reverence for God should be a healthy motivator that causes you to respond no matter the time or the place.

Healthy Motivators	Unhealthy Motivators
■ He is Holy	■ I'm supposed to
■ I get to	■ What's in it for me?
■ I desire to	■ He gave me a new car
■ I can't help but	■ I read in the Bible that it says He will open up windows and pour out a blessing that I don't have room enough to receive
■ He is deserving of it	
■ I was created to	

We also worship God by submitting ourselves unto Him. Surrendering our will, our desires, our life's ambitions, and embracing His will, desires, and plans. He knows the plans for our lives. He is the plan. We shall Worship. We choose to worship. It's a decision. We have a compelling commitment to give our Father worship. In worship we make Him a priority and we place everything aside. The greater your revelation of Him, the greater your worship will be because it's a response to Him.

> *The whole earth will acknowledge the Lord and return to him. All the families of the nations will bow down before him.*
> *Psalm 22:27 NLT*
>
> ⟶
>
> *Jesus replied, "The Scriptures say, 'You must worship the Lord your God and serve only him.'"*
> *Luke 4:8 NLT*

HOW DO WE WORSHIP?

We worship God wholeheartedly with emotion and with fervor. You are excited because you know who He is! You have tasted and seen that He is good and everything in you proclaims and boasts His goodness. Because we come from the creator and we are His handiwork, our bodies and all of who we are worship the one who brought us into existence. You should worship with your heart. Worship isn't solely based on music, songs, or a particular technique. The focus should be on God who we love, on Jesus Christ who made it possible for redemption and reconciliation, and then the Holy Spirit who dwells within us so that we receive all the benefits of being in a royal family. What I have come to find is that if you discover your *why* in something, it can lead you to discover *how*. Remember that your motive will always become your motivator. Once you develop a pure motive of why you worship God, you will begin to discover how you should worship. Development leads to discovery. There is no outline on how it should be done. There is an ongoing non-verbalized debate on what the proper response during corporate worship should be. Hands raised or hands down, lying prostrate or standing, hands clapping or screaming, jumping or stillness, crying or no tears at all, running or shouting. All of it is ridiculous. Again, many have missed it. The expression of worship cannot and should not be limited or restrained before a Holy God. We make it so much about ourselves. Remember what I stated earlier, worship is not defined, it is described. Look to the Old Testament and the New Testament and find countless examples or descriptions of how worship was conducted. You can also find out how God views worship. What makes it acceptable to Him and what is considered unacceptable. I've provided some descriptions and examples of worship.

So the people believed; and when they heard that the Lord had visited the children of Israel and that He had looked on their affliction, then they bowed their heads and worshiped.
Exodus 4:31 NKJV

The man bowed low and worshiped the Lord.
Genesis 24:26 NLT

The twenty-four elders fall down before Him who sits on the throne, and they worship Him who lives forever and ever; and they throw down their crowns before the throne, saying,
Revelation 4:10 AMP

Come, let us worship and bow down. Let us kneel before the Lord our maker, for he is our God.
Psalm 95:6 NLT

And Jehoshaphat bowed his head with his face to the ground, and all Judah and the inhabitants of Jerusalem bowed before the Lord, worshiping the Lord.
2 Chronicles 20:18 NKJV

Bless the Lord, O my soul; And all that is within me, bless His holy name!
Bless the Lord, O my soul, And forget not all His benefits:
Who forgives all your iniquities, Who heals all your diseases,
Who redeems your life from destruction, Who crowns you with
lovingkindness and tender mercies, Who satisfies your mouth with good
things,
So that your youth is renewed like the eagle's.
Psalm 103:1-5 NKJV

Exalt the Lord our God! Bow low before his feet, for he is holy!
Psalm 99:5 NLT

Come let us worship and bow down. Let us kneel before our maker, for he
is our God.
Psalm 95:6 NKJV

Exalt the Lord our God! Bow low before his feet, for he is holy!
Psalm 99:5 NKJV

Come everyone! Clap your hands! Shout to God with joyful praise!
Psalm 47:1 NLT

Lift up your hands toward the sanctuary and praise the Lord.
Psalm 134:2 NLT

Shout to the Lord, all the earth; break out in praise and sing for joy! Sing
your praise to the Lord with the harp, with the harp and melodious song,
with trumpets and the sound of the ram's horn. Make a joyful symphony
before the Lord, the King!
Psalm 98:4-6 NLT

PROPHETIC WORSHIP

Prophetic worship is singing what God is saying for the edification, exhortation and comfort of men. It's an extension of prophecy. Prophetic worship is nothing other than effectively hearing from God, then producing through sound what you believe God is saying through your hearing and seeing... It is prophecy in song. It should be done as He wills and as you yield. It is the Word of the Lord. You are delivering a word from God to the people in song. Prophetic worshipers are sensitive to atmospheres and they recognize when the presence of God is in a place. You must understand the authority that you possess in Christ Jesus in order to truly flow unhindered. By knowing your position in Christ, you are able to operate by faith with an assurance of what God has spoken or shown you. Intercession is strongly associated with prophetic worship. Prayer is an important ingredient for effective worship. You MUST keep a praying spirit. Through a praying spirit, God downloads information and insight to you. It is highly important to pray in the Holy Spirit whenever serving as a leader of worship. The Lord shared this with me:

> "My presence is ever present. I'm omnipresent. What happens is you're spiritually awakened and simply become more aware."

As leaders of worship we have to be aware when leading. It should be worship with a purpose. Intercession also is manifested within the atmosphere and you can experience unusual utterances and groanings through musical sounds. In addition, the Holy Spirit is making intercession for you. You will find that a lot of leaders begin to switch from a song to vowels like oohs and ahs, and maybe even growls, humming, and or even weeping. It is a part of intercession. Do not be afraid when you spontaneously feel led to do things that seem out of your "norm" because the Holy Spirit will use that to break up atmospheres and it could cause the people to open up in worship response. It breaks the hold of the enemy. That is why it is so important to be delivered from people. You have to set your face like flint before the people. Always remember that you should be aware of their response but not dependent on their approval. Their response or lack thereof could cause you to become disobedient to those spontaneous intercessory promptings. I explain intercessory praise and worship a little later.

> *For the Lord God will help Me; Therefore, I will not be disgraced; Therefore I have set my face like a flint, And I know that I will not be ashamed.*
> *Isaiah 50:7 NKJV*

> *Likewise, the Spirit also helps us in our weaknesses. For we do not know what we should pray for as we ought, but the Spirit Himself makes intercession for us with groanings which cannot be uttered. Now He who searches the hearts knows what the mind of the Spirit is, because He makes intercession for the saints according to the will of God.*
> *Romans 8:25-26 NKJV*

A lot of prophetic vessels find themselves gifted in releasing songs. The Holy Spirit is a singing Spirit and songs are always flowing out. God sings over us! In fact, many will say I heard this, or I heard a song that would have fit perfectly in that worship moment. I believe all worship leaders should operate in prophetic worship. Remember everything is as the Holy Spirit wills. You may be led to prophecy in song, there may be a melody given, a rhea word, a logos word in song, a spontaneous gesture to be done, then a declaration to solidify it in the spiritual realm, or even warfare. 1 Corinthians 14:15 tells us that we should sing with the spirit. The amplified version says this:

> *Then what am I to do? I will pray with the spirit [by the Holy Spirit that is within me] and I will pray with the mind [using words I understand]; I will sing with the spirit [by the Holy Spirit that is within me] and I will sing with the mind [using words I understand].*
> *1 Corinthians 14:15 AMP*

Both are acceptable and appropriate for communication and worship to the Lord. It is important to know the Word of God. We must study the word of God to know God's character and to develop God's characteristics. So, if the Word describes us in direct communication with God with the Spirit by our heavenly language then it is the same with singing with the Spirit. God's word is a sure prophecy.

Purpose of Prophetic Worship

The purpose of prophetic worship is to edify, exhort and comfort people so that God can be glorified. Prophetic is intended to perform. God may use it to deliver, set free, challenge, reward, promote, reveal, or even correct but it all should be for the sole purpose of meeting the present need that is in an atmosphere. It is so important to discern the voice of God, but to also walk in obedience because you never know what is at stake when you consider the lives and destinies of people. As Prophetic praise and worship leaders, you can be classified as Atmosphere Shifters, but you must know the authority that you possess in Christ. Prophetic worship can be used by God to completely transform lives.

Your ever-evolving prayer life and worship life will not only keep you close to the throne of God it will unlock more of His gifts for you. Worship and praying in the spirit unlock the door to the prophetic anointing. Many prophetic vessels are at their very core worshipers. In His presence, He is present, and He is speaking. Answers will come, direction, guidance, strategy, healing, deliverance, comfort, love and fullness of joy from that place in His presence.

> *You will show me the path of my life; In Your presence is fullness of joy;*
> *In You right hand there are pleasures forevermore.*
> *Psalm 16:11 NKJV*

It takes hunger, faith, and practice to prophetically worship.

> *Pursue [this] love [with eagerness, make it your goal], yet earnestly desire and cultivate the spiritual gifts [to be used by believers for the benefit of the church], but especially that you may prophesy [to foretell the future, to speak a new message from God to the people].*
> *1 Corinthians 14:1 AMP*

PROPHETIC WORSHIP VS. SPONTANEOUS WORSHIP

Spontaneous Worship is best described as unplanned, impulsive, and impromptu. It is an unwritten song or melody. The singers didn't practice it at rehearsal. The band didn't have it listed on planning center. There are many expressions of it I'm finding. From singing scripture, making declarations, or even transforming a familiar song into something completely unscripted…it's all spontaneous. Spontaneous Worship, powerful, extremely creative and heartfelt is an extension of praise and worship. It is your heart to God. While prophetic worship is God's heart to us, His people. Most spontaneity originates from your heart. It's your heart's cry or utterance. This type of worship can be Holy Spirit inspired or can be simply your adoration to God forming a new song. There are countless new songs birthed out of the creativity of our thanksgiving and remembrance. Spontaneous Worship is a strategic segue into a prophetic flow. It definitely serves its purpose. It's where God takes you off the script and then He can either allow you to improve the scene or breathe fresh lyrics into you and create a whole new scene. It is a place where you can always find a river; which flows from the throne of God and of the lamb as mentioned in Revelation 22:1 NKJV.

> *Oh, sing to the Lord a new song! Sing to the Lord, all the earth. Sing to the Lord, bless His name; Proclaims the good news of is salvation from day to day. Declare His glory among the nations, His wonders among all people. For the Lord is great and greatly to be praised; He is to be feared above all gods. For all the gods of the people are idols, But the Lord made the heavens. Honor and majesty are before Him; Strength and beauty are in His sanctuary. Give to the Lord, O families of the peoples, Give to the Lord glory and strength. Give to the Lord the glory due His name; Bring an offering, and come into His courts. Oh, worship the Lord in the beauty of holiness! Tremble before Him, all the earth.*
> *Psalm 96:1-9 NKJV*

Prophetic Worship is when you speak or sing God's word, or what the Lord is saying during worship for the setting. It can be spontaneous, totally new, or it could be structured and organized. We can NOT limit God and determine how He wants to move. We just have to be willing and obedient to be used. God always wants to meet His people during worship.

For anyone that desires to really cultivate the prophetic, these are the steps that I use to start that process:

- Prayer/Fasting: to gain power and be in alignment with the perfect will of God.
- Set aside intimate time to commune with God in prayer and worship.

- Have a reverence and fear for the Lord.
- Discern the voice of God. How does He speak to you?
- Begin to monitor what you put in your ear gate (what you hear) and eye gate (what you see).
- Practice (sing in the spirit often, sing songs of adoration to the Lord, read a scripture and then sing the scripture, singing is a great way to meditate on scripture).
- Eliminate fear.
- Be released by leadership to operate. Honor leadership. Know the guidelines and restrictions for the house in which you serve.
- Get a worship mentor!
- You NEED the anointing!
- Be obedient!
- Use your FAITH! Take RISKS!
- GO FORTH!

Remember it is just like giving a prophetic word. It is filtered through a human vessel and it can be off. Do not look for the approval of man because what God gives you may be for 1 not 100.

> Because the Sovereign Lord helps me, I will not be disgraced. Therefore, I have set my face like a stone, determined to do His will. And I know that I will not be put to shame.
> Isaiah 50:7 NLT

Nothing you do in God's name will ever be in vain or be overlooked. You will not be ashamed or humiliated. He just wants the obedience and trust. Can you move in obedience when what you're ministering prophetically is for the 1 and not the 99? Do **NOT** be afraid to step out. God can and will show up. There will always be a demonstration. The Spirit of the Lord comes to act out what has been commanded from God. When God stamps you, Heaven responds. The songs you release should also be judged by the house.

> *Let two or three prophets speak, and let the others judge.*
> *1 Corinthians 14:29 NKJV*

As prophetic worshipers, it is easy to get frustrated because you know God was in a place or that you heard properly and delivered it properly, but they did not respond. Do not allow this place to get you in the flesh. Remember, when the response doesn't come, that you are operating in an extension of prophecy. They are rejecting the voice of God, not you. You should always have the motive of seeking to please God through obedience. If the reaction of the people is your focal point, then you have taken your eyes off of the One who sent you. Begin to go seek training from a mature Prophet or Prophetic vessel in your local church and begin developing your gift. Spending time privately articulating what God shows you or speaks to you will assist in the perfecting of your gift and help you move in confidence as you continue to walk in obedience.

Here are some tips for you as you begin to move more into the Prophetic!

- **Tip #1.** Remember who you are doing it for. It should be for God's glory.
- **Tip #2.** Get delivered from people. Do not allow the response to determine you going forth. The response can be deceitful so trust the Holy Spirit's leading.
- **Tip #3.** Flow as the Holy Spirit wills. Decipher how He would desire you to flow. The flow today may be different than tomorrow. The needs in the room change.
- **Tip #4.** Do not forget the purpose of prophetic worship *mentioned above*.
- **Tip #5.** The anointing is what breaks the yoke of bondage and sets people free so seek after the anointing.
- **Tip #6.** Don't get so consumed with trying to create a flow that you forget to have Christ-centered worship.
- **Tip #7.** It is not about you.

Remember that there are hindrances in every atmosphere that do not want the spirit of the Lord to be in control. Prayer and intercession are needed. Just like anything in the prophetic, submit to the Lordship of Jesus Christ and the leadership of your local house and the House Prophet. Have the words you release be tested. Don't be afraid of chastening. Correction produces integrity in you and can help you to develop accuracy. God corrects those whom He loves.

INTERCESSORY PRAISE & WORSHIP WARFARE

When you begin to discover the depths of intercession you will learn that prayer is not the only way to stand in the gap for someone or something. I read a book entitled, *Possessing the Gates of the Enemy.* This book enlightened me to the power of militant intercession but also to a concept of intercessory praise. It was so amazing because God had already been allowing me to flow and be effective in intercession through praise and worship. I was finding that a lot of my warfare would be songs unto the Lord or dancing or treading. I really did not have any knowledge, but I had victories. In my development as a worship leader, this form of intercession has become such a beautiful and effective tool. I desire to expose you to this knowledge. It will change your perspective of how you minister before the people and also how you approach your personal prayer, praise and worship time. The thought of prophetic gestures is more common now in the body of Christ but there has not been any identity or insight brought to this idea of warring in praise and worship as intercession. Intercessory Praise is defined as praise that intercedes or stands in the gap for another.

Many do not know the depths of praise and worship and what it is designed to do for the believer and for the kingdom of darkness. Praise and worship are more than just songs. Praise is not just a fast tempo song and worship is more than a slow tempo song. Psalm 149 speaks to the power of praise.

Hallelujah! Praise the Lord! It's time to sing to God a brand-new song so that all his holy people will hear how wonderful he is! May Israel be enthused with joy because of him, and may the sons of Zion pour out their joyful praises to their King. Break forth with dancing! Make music and sing God's praises with the rhythm of drums! For he enjoys his faithful lovers. He adorns the humble with his beauty and he loves to give them the victory. His godly lovers triumph in the glory of God, and their joyful praises will rise even while others sleep. God's high and holy praises fill their mouths, for their shouted praises are their weapons of war! These warring weapons will bring vengeance on every opposing force and every resistant power- to bind kings with chains and rulers with iron shackles. Praise-filled warriors will enforce the judgement- doom decreed against their enemies. This is the glorious honor he gives to all godly lovers. Hallelujah! Praise the Lord!

Psalm 149 TPT

The Psalmist has a revelation that praise is a great weapon of war. The weapons of our warfare are not carnal, but they are natural things that manifest great victory. It is something about esteeming Jesus Christ to the highest seat that allows Him to show Himself mighty by defeating every opposition that is against Him and you.

The corporate worship of God in church is a form of spiritual warfare. We do not gather out of routine just to say that we had church. It is the Kingdom. There is a war going on in the heavenly realm. The power of praise and worship binds the enemy. Praise also serves as a way to stand in the gap or intercede for others for deliverance and breakthrough to take place. David was used in intercessory praise when he ministered through an instrument for King Saul.

> *So it came about that whenever the [evil] spirit from God was on Saul, David took a harp and played it with his hand; so Saul would be refreshed and be well and the evil spirit would leave him.*
> *1 Samuel 16:23 AMP*

I have actually lived this scripture. I was assisting in deliverance for a woman. The intercessors were praying and identifying by the insight of The Holy Spirit, which evil spirits were at work and began to precede with deliverance. Let me be clear and state that the name above every name Jesus Christ is a powerful name and at that name demons must bow and flee. We know that. I did notice that there was strong resistance because of the agreement or allegiance that the woman had with the spirits. I was instructed to worship. I began to immediately sing praises to Jesus and worship Him through song and the woman was released. I believe God demonstrated His supernatural power because He was esteemed high in that moment. It was so powerful, and I began to understand that when praises are in my mouth it is as a sharp sword devouring the enemy. I encourage you to use this method whenever you get into spiritual opposition. Singing praises and singing scripture will strengthen your spirit man and bind the works of the enemy. Satan understands the power of music and of praise and worship. In fact, some believe that he was once the worship leader of heaven. Ezekiel 28:13b NKJV says: "*The workmanship of*

your timbrels and pipes was prepared for you on the day you were created."
The book, *The Rebirth of Music,* explains it this way:

> *Lucifer has tambourines and pipes built into his hands and body and had the ability to play these pipes or tambourines extremely well. It is definitely clear that Lucifer excelled in music and that it was part of him. The Bible refers to pipes, plural, meaning there was more than one.*

Isaiah 14:11a KJV says, *"Thy pomp is brought down to the grave, and the noise of thy viols."* Viols are a six-stringed instrument which represents all stringed instruments. So, the total spectrum of instruments that we play today except for electronic instruments were built into Lucifer's body. He could play them all.

The Word of God says this in Psalm 22:3 NKJV,

"But You are holy, enthroned in the praises of Israel." When we praise God, He inhabits or enters our praises, and His power overwhelms the power of the enemy. He is a mighty God, and Satan cannot match His strength. Light will dispel the darkness through God's entering into our praise.

This aspect of worshiping God enabled Paul and Silas to be set free from the enemy and dispel his power. Acts 16:25 NKJV says, *"But at midnight Paul and Silas were praying and singing hymns to God, and the prisoners were listening to them."*

There are seven Hebrew words for praise that can be used in different times during praise and worship.

1. *Halal.* To be boastful, excited; tremendous explosion of enthusiasm in the act of praising (the word *hallelujah* is from the word *halal*).

    Praise the Lord, all you nations. Praise him, all you people of the earth.
    Psalm 117:1 NLT

2. **Yadah.** To thank, to give public acknowledgment to, to extend the hand, to worship with raised hands.

    Then the Levites from the clans of Kohath and Korah stood to praise the Lord, the God of Israel, with a very loud shout. Early the next morning the army of Judah went out into the wilderness of Tekoa. On the way Jehoshaphat stopped and said, "Listen to me, all you people of Judah and Jerusalem! Believe in the Lord your God, and you will be able to stand firm. Believe in his prophets, and you will succeed." After consulting the people, the king appointed singers to walk ahead of the army, singing to the Lord and praising him for his holy splendor. This is what they sang: "Give thanks to the Lord; his faithful love endures forever!"
    2 Chronicles 20:19-21 NLT

3. **Barak.** To bless, to bow, to kneel in adoration.

    Let all that I am praise the Lord; with my whole heart, I will praise his holy name. Let all that I am praise the Lord; may I never forget the good things he does for me.
    Psalm 103:1-2 NLT

4. **Zamar.** To touch the string, to make music to God. This is a musical verb for praise.

Praise the Lord with the harp; Make melody to Him with an instrument of ten strings.
Psalm 33:2 NKJV

5. **Shabach.** To speak well of in a high and befitting way. It means to address in a loud tone, to shout, to command triumph.

Oh, clap your hands, all you peoples! Shout to God with the voice of triumph!
Psalm 47:1 NKJV

6. **Tephillah.** Intercession for someone, supplication, a hymn.

I will bring them to my holy mountain of Jerusalem and will fill them with joy in my house of prayer. I will accept their burnt offerings and sacrifices, because my Temple will be called a house of prayer for all nations.
Isaiah 56:7 NLT

7. **Towdah.** Thanksgiving; also involves the extension of the hand in thanksgiving; to give the sacrifice of praise.

But giving thanks is a sacrifice that truly honors me. If you keep to my path, I will reveal to you the salvation of God."
Psalm 50:23 NLT

Praise, prayer and intercession are all intertwined, and you will notice that out of your place of prayer will come praise. Prayer brings insight, strength and refreshing to the believer and praise brings victory which explains why the enemy tries so hard to prevent you from having a thriving prayer life and a vibrant life of praise. God inhabits the praises of His people and His dwelling causes anything opposed to Him to cease to operate. The enemy also seeks to attack the worship leader with a spirit of heaviness. The spirit of heaviness brings depression, sorrow, grief, worry, anxiousness, procrastination, doubt, and unbelief. It seeks to rob your joy and reduce your fire for the things of God to affect your fellowship with the Lord. Isaiah 61:3 NKJV says, *"To console those who mourn in Zion, To give them beauty for ashes, The oil of joy for mourning, The garment of praise for the spirit of heaviness; that they may be called trees of righteousness, The planting of the Lord, that He may be glorified."* As believers we can seek God to give us the oil of joy and to give us a garment of praise. Just as with any natural garment, it is used for shelter or covering your natural body, we use the garment of praise to cover your spirit and provide shelter. Intercessory praise is an effectual weapon to keep the strong man from blinding the eyes of those who need to receive the Gospel of Jesus Christ.

I have listed some other weapons and tools that are effective and powerful in engaging warfare and intercession.

Walking and Marching - Produces a deliverance and breakthrough. Joshua and his troops marched around the walls and following the Lord's instruction they saw victory. Marching is a powerful tool used in the corporate worship setting. There is a unity that can be accomplished to see victory in marching. This is also a prophetic gesture and can be used to be a foresight of what is to come.

I promise you what I promised Moses: "Wherever you set foot, you will be on land I have given you. - Joshua 1:3 NLT

Treading - An aggressive march. Treading includes actually stopping the power of the enemy. We have authority to tread through Christ Jesus!

Listen carefully: I have given you authority [that you now possess] to tread on serpents and scorpions, and [the ability to exercise authority] over all the power of the enemy (Satan); and nothing will [in any way] harm you.
Luke 10:19 NLT
Through God we will do valiantly, For it is He who shall tread down our enemies.
Psalm 108:13 NKJV

Singing - New songs that are specifically used to break the chains of bondage and bind the hand of the enemy. Songs of praise that exalt Jesus Christ used for war. Many underestimate the power of these songs. This type of singing is not a prophetic song or a spontaneous song it is a STRATEGIC song that is used to exalt and bring esteem to the Name greater than any name, Jesus. What I mean by that is, these types of songs are not for the edification, exhortation and comfort of the body of Christ, these songs are for war and specifically to engage in battle. They are for the spiritual realm not the gathering of the body. He shows His mighty power and gives us victory over our enemies. It is very effective. That is why we have so many songs now that declare, "This is how I fight my battles, or my praise is a weapon, or my shout is a weapon!"

You shall have a song as in the night when a holy festival is kept, And gladness of heart as when one goes with a flute, To come into the mountain of the Lord, To the mighty One of Israel. The Lord will cause His glorious voice to be heard, And how the descent of His arm, With the indignation of His anger And the flame of a devouring fire, With scattering, tempest, and hailstones.
Isaiah 30: 29-30 NKJV

Clapping - The word *clap* in this passage is *teqae*: clang, smite, strike. Ezekiel 6:11a NKJV says: "Thus says the Lord God: "Pound your fists and stamp your feet." Clapping in the Bible is associated not only with praise but also with warfare. Clapping is one means of breaking yokes.

Oh, clap your hands, all you peoples! Shout to God with the voice of triumph!
Psalm 47:1 NKJV

Shouting: Battle/War Cry

Then the men of Judah gave a shout; and as the men of Judah shouted, it happened that God struck Jeroboam and all Israel before Abijah and Judah
2 Chronicles 13:15 NKJV

2

The Worshiper

The Worshiper is any person, place, or thing who has a revelation of worship and does it. Studying the word of God, you will find that not only people have the ability and capacity to worship God but so do angels, creatures, trees, flowers, oceans and rivers, animals, the sun, the moon, the stars, and the sky. Everything in the earth, over the earth and under the earth recognize the authority and power in the One who is called El Elyon. We are all called to be worshippers. Worshipers have a holy passion for Jesus. We were created for the very purpose of worship. We worship to give reverence and obedience. The spirit within us compels us to worship. It sounds simple, right? Just get a revelation on worship and do it. I believe it is important to the true worshiper that Jesus mentioned in John 4 because that is the only worshiper that God truly finds pleasing and acceptable. As worshipers, our responsibility is to respond to God, and it happens best out of having a personal relationship with Jesus Christ. Relationships are securely built on trust. True worship requires a personal connection, admiration and reverence. That kind of heart position cannot be taught but must be developed. It must be experienced, encountered and engaged continually for this true revelation to be revealed.

This reality of the worshiper is so important because it provides insight on what's being experienced in most corporate church services. The body of Christ lacks relationship and intimacy with God, and as a result their worship suffers. You could be experiencing division before the call to worship even begins. I promise, if you go to a church service and you ask the Lord to show you what's in the atmosphere, He will truly do just that. I believe there is a remnant of people God is raising up that love Him without restraint, and neither location nor setting will prevent their worship expression. In my experience, you have people who gather together but not necessarily in unity. The scriptures tell us in Psalm 133 how good and pleasant it is for brothers to live and dwell in unity. I believe that it is also good and pleasant for brothers to *worship* in unity. Most times the free flow of God's glory is hindered because there are several types of worshiper's present. Everyone has an agenda or a motive, their *why* they gathered, whether they realize it or not. When you read this, I want to encourage you with this scripture.

> *So now there is no condemnation for those who belong to Christ Jesus.*
> *Romans 8:1 NLT*

47

Four Types of Worshipers
The Critic
The Performer
The Religious
The Pure in Heart

THE CRITIC

First, you have the critic also known as the spectator. They do not come to participate but rather to spectate. There is no genuine interest of joining in with the angels. They are a huge blockage and a nuisance to the intercessor. The critic is the type of worshiper that is focused on the top-ten playlist being sung during the corporate worship time. They are assessing the song leader, and in their mind, they are thinking, "she/he could have done that better," "Ugh! They did not hit that note right," "this song again." They are so distracted, and they lack revelation tremendously. They are judgmental and often vocal about what they liked/didn't like. They gauge the anointing by the way the music made them feel. They lack true connection during corporate worship time because they are too busy assessing the atmosphere and prone to look for error. When they sense a tough atmosphere, they don't intercede and pray for the enemy to be bound and for God's people to be free in their worship, they instead are the ones with their heads cocked to the side, looking puzzled and allowing their minds to roam and zoom in on what needs to be better and changed. What they fail to realize is that their immaturity and critiques hinder the atmosphere. Such behavior robs the critic of an authentic worship encounter with the true and living God because they do not have a level of expectation, they just have their so-called information. They often leave the way they came. What I have always found intriguing about the critic is that they are critical of the sermon, pastors, their boss, colleagues, family and friends. Remember Sunday is just one day out of a seven-day week. One day can be a clear indicator of what your other six days look like.

THE PERFORMER

The performer is all about having an audience. They strive to be the main attraction and seek attention with the hope of feeling validated. In their opinion, they are the only carriers of glory...if you ask them. Their focus has been removed from the true purpose of worship, and now their sole focus is on being seen and creating an image that it appears like they deserve a real intimate relationship with Christ. The performer is completely aware of this, but they are more consumed with the public's viewpoint and pseudo approval versus God's viewpoint and God's approval. It's the "I want to sing on the praise team and dance on the dance team" type mentality. This type of mentality is very self-centered and takes the focus off of Christ-centered worship. The performer operates in pride and often gets confused with the religious worshiper. The performer is the one that says they praise God but has yet to seek God to find the character and heart of God. You normally see the performer in operation when they are struggling with people-pleasing.

There are so many people who have experienced rejection and abandonment. Without proper deliverance and healing taking place, these cancer cells will grow and form many tumors. Fear, acceptance from people, and trust issues develop. It is extremely important as a worshiper to allow God to truly uproot those things out of your life. The trick of the enemy is to have you focus on the audience of many instead of the approval of one. A performer consciously, or not, goes before people and they want to be validated. They want to be accepted. Loved. Praised. They want everyone to see the appearance of holiness and worship. They are literally actors in the spiritual realm. They do not invest any time cultivating a personal relationship with the Lord, but when corporate worship starts, its lights, camera, action. The performer tends to be guarded in his presence, and then in corporate settings they exaggerate their expression. In order to break out of a performer you must understand why this type of worship is wrong. Worship is not about you; it is about the One who created you. It is for God's glory. You can receive freedom if you first begin to pursue a vulnerable, transparent prayer and worship life. Fear must be renounced, and healing has to take place in order for the performer to accept that they are worthy of God's love and can be true to themselves and worship in truth. God loves you!

This just came to mind. You find that a lot of people who perform in His presence are really hurting and need healing. The root of the performance, or "acting," is that they don't want to be too open or real because then it will expose the things hidden in them, and fear of getting hurt or being rejected due to their issues. They blame God for events that have happened in their lives. Many believers still can't grasp the concept of God being their Creator and Father. I urge you to not develop such an awe-view of God that you cannot embrace the intimate nature of our God. Yes, He set the sun and moon in the sky, but God also counted the hairs on your head.

> *Indeed, the very hairs of your head are numbered. Do not be afraid; you are far more valuable than many sparrows.*
> *Luke 12:7 AMP*

I feel led to say this. God is a loving God, but He is also just. His ways are not like our ways and you must let go of that grudge toward God in order to experience a new level of intimacy and healing. You cannot get healing from someone you reject. So yes, you are singing the songs and clapping, but you are angry. Let that anger go. Let those thoughts go.

Challenge questions to ask yourself if you identify with The Performer

- What is your inner expression of worship?
- Is your heart connected?
- You can lift your hands, but have you lifted your heart?
- What is the posture of your heart during worship?
- What is the motive of your heart during worship?
- Is your motive to give Him glory and honor Him, or is it for the benefit of what He can do for you?

Ways to kill The Performer in You

- Acknowledge that God does not honor performances.
- Repent.
- Renounce the spirit of fear and distrust.
- Say this aloud: I renounce all fear, doubt and unbelief in the name of Jesus!
- Ask the Holy Spirit to heal you of the insecurity in you that seeks attention and recognition.
- Ask for the Holy Spirit to heal you of damage that makes you guarded in His presence.
- Fast to get your spirit revived in the truth of God.
- Read your Bible daily.
- Jot down scriptures to profess daily over yourself.
- Start reading Psalms and Proverbs.
- Cultivate a private worship life where you are vulnerable and transparent in His presence.

Scripture Declaration:

Create a clean heart for me, God; and put a new, faithful spirit deep inside me! Psalm 51:10 CEB

THE RELIGIOUS WORSHIPER

When you think of the religious worshiper, think bland and routine, worship lacking power and fire, and most importantly, deep connection. They have memorized worship sets. They run at the right time. They holler, scream, lift their hands, but no real fruit is exhibited. The religious, and performer are different because the religious worshiper hasn't been exposed to the knowledge of truth. Most times they've encountered false teaching and have no idea what true and proper worship really is, so they just mimic what they've seen or what's been instilled in them. You'll find religious worshipers are really desiring freedom and knowledge so they can experience the fullness. It's like I hear people say all the time, "I want to change, I just don't know how'. They really mean that. I grew up in church and I can say confidently that no one had a true revelation of what true and proper worship was. I came up in a very expressive, charismatic context where getting filled with the Holy Spirit was an hour-long tarrying process of repeating Jesus until tongues flowed out, and the trashcan was in place for when you coughed up your demons, and where if you did not shout or dance you were not authentic. However, it was the same context where sexual misconduct was present, gossip and unrighteousness functioned unbothered.

Saying that to say, I was religious. I was truly under the impression that you could live any way and God was okay with that. I wasn't taught the truth concerning confession, repentance, and grace. So, when it came to my worship, I literally did what I saw done. It was passed down like a rite of passage. There was no real teaching or revelation. I believe those who grew up in church, or had exposure to church, were at some point or another religious. There is no escaping that. Think in terms of the Bible, there are many examples of a religious people and God had to encounter them and set order and tell them who He was and describe what it meant to respond to that. I urge parents to be mindful of the truths you instill in your children and the methods in which you present truths to them. You could be grooming a religious lineage. As young children you learn quickly that you cannot go higher than your parents are willing to go. As a child you are under that covering. Let's pray for that right now!

Ways to Kill the Religious Worshiper in You

- Desire to change.
- Repent for any unconfessed sin. Sin is a hindrance for true worship.
- Get delivered from the spirit of religion.
- Read your Bible. The more you read about God's character the more you will develop it.
- Get an understanding of your position in Christ.
- Develop a hunger for a deeper relationship with God.
- Pray.
- Fast, which brings you into alignment with God.
- Ask the Holy Spirit what to reveal to you about worship.
- Read books to stir your desire for God and His glory.
- Go into a worship setting and desire to connect with God, not to compare to tradition.
- Pursue authenticity when you worship at home.
- Prayer for generations.

Prayer for the Religious Worshiper:

Father forgive me for the spirit of religion that I have operated in. I recognize that I am religious, and I desire to be changed. I know You desire relationship and not religion. You hate religion. I want to hate what You hate and love what You love. I desire to be set free from this spirit that has been wrapped around my neck suffocating me from the true authentic relationship You desire with me. I pray for Your forgiveness. I ask that the blood of Jesus cleanses me from anything not like You that would hinder me or block me from getting closer to You. I close all doors and I surrender to the work of the Holy Spirit in my life. Help me Holy Spirit to understand the heart of God. Teach me how to truly worship God not with my lips or on Sundays but with my life, with my heart. I want to encounter the fullness of what You have to offer. I no longer wish to be bound to tradition and pass down rites of passage that hold no power and don't display love. I want who You are. I want to know what is acceptable and pleasing to You. I receive You now. I believe that You are stepping in now to help me and bring answers and restore relationship. I welcome You Holy God. Take me deeper until I know the complete expression of Your love and power.

In Jesus Name,
Amen.

THE PURE IN HEART

Shout with joy to the Lord, all the earth! Worship the Lord with gladness.
Come before him, singing with joy. Acknowledge that the Lord is God!
He made us, and we are his. We are his people, the sheep of his pasture.
Enter his gates with thanksgiving; go into his courts with praise. Give
thanks to him and praise his name. For the Lord is good. His unfailing
love continues forever, and his faithfulness continues to each generation.
Psalm 100 NLT

Let's just say that the Pure in Heart live by this passage of scripture. They do not have to be pumped up or persuaded to glorify God. They already know He is worthy to receive glory and honor. The Pure in Heart possess an awareness of God. They are in constant pursuit of Him because they recognize that they still have very little knowledge of this Almighty God. Wholehearted is an adjective that describes their response of worship. Being in a constant place of surrender, provides them with unlimited emotion towards Jesus Christ. They comprehend the power of what praise and worship does to the enemy and his schemes. They love exalting the Name that is above every name. Their worship is so expressive, but it does not compare to how they view God in their hearts. The very thought of Him brings them to their knees. To clarify, the pure in heart worshiper is not perfect at all. In fact, they may very well need lots of work and fruit, BUT what separates them is their dependence on God. They recognize that they need the Father in every way. It is no secret that they enter into His courts with thanksgiving and His courts with praise.

The Pure in Heart are full of reverence and revelation. They understand the true meaning of worship and they dedicate their lives to glorifying God. They delight in worshiping Jesus. These are the people that on Monday, Tuesday, Wednesday, Thursday, Friday and Saturday they rejoice in the Lord. They carry a spirit of gratefulness. These are the people who have been forgiven much and so they love much. They understand if it had not been for God being on their side, fighting their battles and making ways for them, they would be nothing. They have the joy of their salvation and they rekindle the fire within their bellies daily because they never want to lose that closeness with the Lord.

Who, then, ascends into the presence of the Lord? And who has the privilege of entering into God's Holy Place? Those who are clean—whose works and ways are pure, whose hearts are true and sealed by the truth, those who never deceive, whose words are sure. They will receive the Lord's blessing and righteousness given by the Savior-God. They will stand before God, for they seek the pleasure of God's face, the God of Jacob.
Psalm 24:3-6 TPT

The scripture is very clear that those who are clean and whose hearts are true ascend into that Holy Place or the Holy of Holies. That place is where answers are and the shalom of God. The very essence of Jesus is found in that place.

God blesses those whose hearts are pure, for they will see God.
Matthew 5:8 NLT

When you allow a pure heart to be developed in you, your worship is always acceptable before the Lord because your motive and intent is in alignment with God's word. You are granted access to see more of God. We underestimate the beauty of a pure heart. God reveals mysteries and adds to you when He knows you have a pure heart because you are not after selfish gain. You will not take credit for the miracles, signs and wonders working through you. You wear the cloak of humility as a badge of honor.

What we as believers should understand is that because of sin and being born into iniquity, we need to learn how to worship God. What I mean by that statement is, your flesh and body do not have a desire to worship, but your spirit does. We simply have to be taught purity and worship from the Holy Spirit. He knows what pleases the Father.

Prayer for the Pure in Heart Worshiper:

For I have tasted and seen of the goodness of You Lord. I love everything You are, and I thank You for being my God. I thank You for the purpose of worship and for revealing Your heart to me. I pray Father that I will forever have a pure heart before You. Continue to create in me a clean heart and renew a right spirit within me that I may forever please You and honor You with my life and my worship before You. I just want to please You. I pray that every weapon formed against me to deter me and distract me not prosper according to Your word so that I may walk in victory. I thank You Lord for enabling me to maintain a pure heart before You. That is what I desire Lord. May I forever glorify Your name no matter what I experience or come up against all the glory belongs to You.
In Jesus Name,
Amen.

My Life Counts

The Worshiper has a mandate from heaven to live a lifestyle that is reflective of worship. When you do not live purposefully to glorify God in your daily life then how can you truly worship? Does He just love us on Sundays and Wednesdays? No. So we should make it our mission to honor Him daily with our hearts and our lives. What you wear, how you treat your colleagues, your boss, your spouse, what you watch, consume in your body, participate in, what you say, and what you think, what you meditate on, all of it is worship.

And so, dear brothers and sisters, I plead with you to give your bodies to God because of all he has done for you. Let them be a living and holy sacrifice-- the kind he will find acceptable. This is truly the way to worship him.
Romans 12:1 NLT

The amplified version states
...To present your bodies [dedicating all of yourselves, set apart] as a living sacrifice, holy and well-pleasing to God, which is your rational (logical, intelligent) act of worship.

Everyone Worships Something

What are you worshiping? As believers we have placed so much emphasis on corporate worship, but many in the body of Christ have not mastered a life reflective of worship. We worship God by living a life of righteousness and loving as He loves. Worship is described by how we live our lives. We give of ourselves as God has given to us freely.

Any form of worship (reverence) that is not Christ-centered/God-focused is idol worship. We can make anything an idol. It doesn't have to be carved out of wood for it to be an idol. We can idolize our churches, pastors, families, spouses, jobs, money, material possessions, social media, our gifts, our callings and even our purpose. Anytime you're not willing to submit something under the authority of God it has become an idol.

> *And whatever you do, do it heartily, as to the Lord and not to men, knowing that from the Lord you will receive the reward of the inheritance; for you serve the Lord Christ. But he who does wrong will be repaid for what he has done, and there is no partiality.*
> *Colossians 3:23-25 NKJV*

Isaiah talks about how the people in Israel were worshiping idols/false gods and they would cry out to them. God referenced them as worthless idols because an idol can't redeem you, save you, cleanse you, purify you, comfort you, correct you, heal you, deliver you, set you free, or bless you, only the TRUE AND LIVING GOD can do such things. How can something dead bring you life? Is God as valuable to you as you profess that He is? These are questions you should ask yourself often. I think a common mistake is for the believer to assume just because they are in a good season and their relationship is going well with Christ, does not mean that you cannot ever find yourself creating idols or getting distracted. Self-deception is real. It has become revealed knowledge to me that God despises idols because they are harmful to His children. False worship and false allegiance open the door to demonic influence and wickedness in your life. It seeps in through a simple television show or a meaningless thought and is designed to pull you further away from God and to ultimately bring about spiritual death. Be very cautious of what is allowed int o your ear and eye gate. Remove symbols that have evil meaning and commit to being a true child of the one true and living God, making covenant with Him only.

> *Keep your heart with all diligence, For out of it spring the issues of life.*
> *Proverbs 4:23 NKJV*
>
> *Wherever your treasure is, there the desires of your heart will also be.*
> *Matthew 6:21 NLT*
>
> *And so the Lord says, "These people say they are mine. They honor me with their lips, but their hearts are far from me. And their worship of me is nothing but man-made rules learned by rote.*
> *Isaiah 29:13 NLT*

Ways to get back to Christ-centered worship

- Repent if you haven't placed Him first.
- Make a commitment to have Him number one in your life.
- We are transformed by the renewing of our mind, so now you need to renew your mind on the way you think about Him and worship.
- Reading the Word of God.
- Putting it into action.

- Have a heart of thanksgiving and praise.
- Remembering what He has done.
- Receiving a revelation of Kingdom and the purpose and power of worship.

Everything starts in the heart

My heart has heard you say, "Come and talk with me." And my heart responds, "Lord, I am coming."
Psalm 27:8 NLT

Everything about us and about worship starts in the heart. Our hearts respond to God first. The Psalmist understood the power of the heart. If your heart is not connected to God, then it is a false expression. That is why believers can sin, repent, and then do it again repeatedly. We always hear preachers say it is because you need to renew your mind concerning the sin. Yes, sure! But you need to change your heart concerning it. *Proverbs 4:23* NKJV tells us, "Keep your heart with all diligence, for out of it spring the issues of life." The heart houses the true identity and perspective of who we really are. And just like with our minds, the heart has to be purified, cleansed, and renewed in order for it to display the likeness and image of Christ. Do not be the worshiper that is so focused on the renewing of your mind that you disregard attention to your heart. Big mistake!

God shared a powerful revelation with me once. He said, *"Sarenina I have to deal with your heart first, then your mind, because your mind is where the issues are being processed but your heart is where the issues were deposited."* When we encounter trauma or experiences, whether good or bad, our hearts receive a deposit. When you serve, love people, or hurt them, it is done out of your heart. It is like a bank account. Just like you can only withdraw what has been deposited naturally, it is the same spiritually. So, if you do not have goodness, grace, compassion, forgiveness, love, and service deposited you cannot withdraw that. You will go into the negative! In allowing God to address the deposits in your heart, He can supernaturally remove the deposits of error and place in His deposits. So that when withdrawn, they yield more dividends. The word instructs us to hide the word in our hearts that we may not sin against Him.

> *Your word I have hidden in my heart, that I might not sin against you.*
> *Psalm 119:11 NKJV*

When we read scripture, we are making deposits in our hearts, so when temptation arises or your flesh desires to react, you will respond with what is in your heart. You can then respond with truth! When lies come, you can withdraw truth from your heart! How amazing is our God! Just writing this makes me rejoice!

3

The Worship Leader

What is a worship leader? A worship leader is a vessel that helps a people to recognize and to respond to the presence of God. The worship leader assists to bring the believer into a place of intimacy, trust, and communion with God in a worship setting. They seek to create an atmosphere for God to dwell and for the recipient to benefit from the move of the Holy Spirit. They are human vessels with a responsibility from Heaven to carry out the assignment of God in the earth concerning worship for His glory. They are not to act alone in this assignment as that is unrealistic for any person to achieve. A worship leader is more than just a gifted musician or a skilled song leader. They are teachers and students, meaning they instruct a people and then they are learning from God all at same time. I had to be the student and teacher simultaneously. You will find many possess worship leadership abilities before being given a title or position. If it is in you, then it is in you. If God chose you, it will be embedded into the very essence of who you are. When I think of how to describe the worship leader, I have to think of my own process. My process was one of constant pruning that has led me closer to Christ and the grace to walk in a boldness like I never thought I could experience. In this chapter, we will dissect the innermost workings of a leader of worship. From the natural to the spiritual, to the relevant and practical, we will explore how to go from a worshiper to the worship leader. First let's lay a foundation.

In being a worship leader, it is of the utmost importance to be a worshipper. One of the prerequisites for worship leadership is a life of prayer and obedience. In leading worship, you will only go as far as your obedience will take you. If we are not able to obey God with the small instructions and nudges, you will never experience the "more" in God and miss the elevation in your life. You have to be obedient in how you lead, what you sing, how you live, your thoughts, obeying His commands, and His rhema word. You have to understand that with obedience comes trust. In Matthew 25:23a NKJV it says, "His lord said to him, 'Well *done,* good and faithful servant; you have been faithful over a few things, I will make you ruler over many things." When we obey God on one level of the anointing He has allotted to us, we will experience more of Him and His presence. At the very essence, prayer is simply communication with God. Your prayer life is essential because it keeps you connected to God. You learn His character, His thoughts, He reveals your heart, and He provides instruction and clarity. Prayer allows you to stay centered and grounded, it puts our own lives in perspective to who God is and who He called us to be.

The biggest benefit of prayer is being connected to the heart of God and experiencing His presence. It is every believer's responsibility to develop a prayer life... but for a worship leader it is mandatory. It cannot be inherited, rather it must be built brick by brick and layer by layer. Communication with God is essential if you are entrusted to go on behalf of God to His people. It is critical that we know what the heart of God is and what He is saying at any moment. Without prayer and obedience working together there is little room for a worship leadership. These two things are foundational.

SUBMISSION IS SAFETY

It is important for worship leaders to be connected to a local house and submitted under proper leadership. Leaders who are chosen by God and have the heart of God will aide in your success, in your character and spiritual development. You can have a mature gift, but you can be immature. When you have leaders who see your gift and your character they can groom and train you to mature in every area of your life, which strengthens you for Kingdom Impact. That comes with submitting your gift under leadership. There's a book called *"I'm Anointed, Yet I'm Covered"* by Jason A. Porter that gives insight as to how to submit your gift under leadership. I recommend you get this book. In *I'm Anointed Yet I'm Covered* author Jason Porter states, "You must realize that Satan opposes any type of order, especially God's divine order. As you connect to a house, there will, or should be accountability within the house.

Accountability will begin to reveal those scars, wounds, and demonic influences that have restricted you from obtaining spiritual liberation. Spiritual liberation is what every believer in Christ should desire. The Shepherd that you are connecting to does matter. You want to connect with a Shepherd who possesses the ability to impart into you through divine revelation and by spiritual discernment from God. I knew it was a must for me to have a Shepherd who hears from God. I understood if my Shepherd heard from God that God would show my Shepherd how to care for me. Many times, sheep become frustrated with their Shepherd because they feel as if the Shepherd does not see what God has placed inside of them. In I Peter 5:6 KJV, the word of God states, *"Humble yourselves, therefore, under the mighty hand of God, that he may exalt you up in due time."* When it is time, the Lord knows how to elevate you to where you need to be. The problem has been that many sheep fail the humility test. To receive your proper honor, you first must master humility. Your idea of humility is not always God's idea of humility. The real humility test is to withstand correction from your Shepherd."

Despite the opinion of others, **every** leader should be a servant, and connected to a local house. Matthew 23:11 NKJV states, *"But he who is greatest among you shall be your servant."*

Being connected to my spiritual leadership positioned me for purpose. It allowed me the proper space to develop my personal relationship with the Lord while providing intentional leadership as well as a safe haven to ask questions, make mistakes, to excel, and to mature. When I became a member of Divine Life Church, I had no clue of what submission was, but because of my heart to truly please God I learned what honor was when it comes to leadership. God began to show me how to trust my spiritual leadership by revealing their hearts to me. Once that revelation came, it was easy to submit because I knew I was connected to leaders who loved my soul more than my gift. In my obedience and choice to submit, I discovered safety and accelerated in the plan of God for my life. Hallelujah! Honestly, I feel so at ease knowing that I'm covered by leaders who are after God's own heart and that recognize the gifts that are on the inside of me. My pastors not only watch after my soul, but they have entrusted me with a platform to go forth with what God has mandated me to do. I strongly encourage worship leaders to submit under a local house. It will change your life and your worship.

A covering will equip you, train you, pray for you, watch for your soul and guide you according to the perfect will of God for your life. Show me a worship leader that isn't submitted to a local house and I will show you someone who isn't being perfected. We need the body of Christ. There is no way you can mature in Christ without community within a local house. If you don't have a covering and you've been going to multiple churches and ministering, but you're not accountable to anyone, then I admonish you to find a local house as soon as possible. There is safety in having a covering. There is safety in submitting your gifts. We don't need performers. We need leaders who are being perfected. We do NOT need wilderness worship leaders!

Scripture References:

But He said, "More than that, blessed are those who hear the word of God and keep it!"
Luke 11:28 NKJV

Thus says the Lord of hosts, the God of Israel: Add your burnt offerings to your sacrifices and eat meat. For I did not speak to your fathers, or command them in the day that I brought them out of the land of Egypt, concerning burnt offerings or sacrifices. But this is what I commanded them, saying, 'Obey My voice, and I will be your God, and you shall be My people. And walk in all the ways that I have commanded you, that it may be well with you.
Jeremiah 7:21-23 NKJV

Seek the Lord and His strength; Seek His face evermore!
I Chronicles 16:11 NKJV

Then you will call upon Me and pray to Me, and I will listen to you. And you will seek Me and find Me, when you search for Me with all your heart.
Jeremiah 29:12-13 NKJV

But you, when you pray, go into your room, and when you have shut your door, pray to your Father who is in the secret place; and your Father who sees in secret will reward you openly. And when you pray, do not use vain repetitions as the heathen do. For they think they will be heard for their many words.
Matthew 6:6-7 NKJV

THE WILDERNESS WORSHIP LEADER

Biblically, we have seen the wilderness referenced as a time of drought, suffering and spiritual attack. The Bible refers to Jesus being led into the wilderness to be tempted by the enemy. The Bible refers to the children of Israel wandering in the wilderness before reaching the land that was promised. Elijah experienced the wilderness as well. I do believe the wilderness as being an intentional place that God is with you. But I also have found that you can be a wanderer in a wilderness that God has not ordained. It manifests itself as a reaction and the action is isolation, detachment, or rebellion.

A wilderness worship leader is a wanderer. They see no value in honoring authority and submitting their gifts to the local body of Christ. They are aware of the gifts and callings over their life, but they ignore God's system and order of being trained and equipped. They are often prideful and if you look even closer, they have experienced church hurt, offense, manipulation and control. They need healing. They have been mishandled and they are wounded. They are the walking dead, but yet are operating. Their effectiveness in the kingdom is not at a level where it should be because they are functioning outside of God's order. So, you find that you are spewing poison and contaminating other ministries. You go and drop atomic bombs and leave. You lack commitment, stability, and correction. You're a freelance agent. You get into a routine of gigging and performing, and in the spiritual realm you're in distress. That's a dangerous place to be in as a worship leader.

If you desire in your heart to be planted in a local church and covered under a spiritual leadership but it just seems that you are unable to truly remain under a covering, it may be a wandering spirit at work. Wilderness worship leaders can easily operate heavily under a vagabond spirit. They run away from being fathered, having suffered abuse and mistreatment from authority and/or spiritual leadership. There is deliverance that needs to take place from the spirit of wandering (vagabond), so you can allow yourself to be planted and experience the fruit of the Holy Spirit in your life. Moving from job to job, church to church, city to city are some key identifiers if you are living with vagabond in operation. Additionally, the wanderer should pray against the spirit of fear and rejection which is designed by the adversary to bring stagnation and delay to your purpose and destiny in Christ Jesus.

I believe we are in a critical time and day where we need true, authentic, and holy leadership. The people who are wandering in the wilderness desire shepherds with integrity and a heart to care and tend to their wounds. We need Shepherds that will not bring judgement but will bring accountability, healing, safety and training.

I caution Shepherds leading from a place outside of God's instruction and order. Do not allow jealousy and pride to put you in a place of corruption with God's things. I encourage you to repent and turn, so that you may be redeemed and washed clean because judgement will be brought into the body of Christ, and God will be seeking answers from those in authority who mishandled the sheep. Sometimes, after being in the wilderness for so long, you feel so lost or so condemned, and your soul is soothed that it's hard to humble yourselves and repent and seek help. Remember God hears the groanings and secret cries of our hearts.

> *And the Holy Spirit helps us in our weakness. For example, we don't know what God wants us to pray for. But the Holy Spirit prays for us with groanings that cannot be expressed in words.*
> *Romans 8:26 NLT*

Be encouraged to know that God is merciful and desires you to return to Him and be back in relationship and obedience with Him. He promised that He wouldn't be angry forever. I believe this is what God is saying right now to the wilderness worship leader:

"Return, faithless Israel, declares the Lord. I will not look on you in anger for I am merciful, declares the Lord; I will not be angry forever. Only acknowledge your guilt, that you rebelled against the Lord your God and scattered your favors among foreigners under every green tree, and that you have not obeyed my voice, declares the Lord. Return, O faithless children, declares the Lord; for I am your master; I will take you, one from a city and two from a family, and I will bring you to Zion. "And I will give you shepherds after my own heart,

who will feed you with knowledge and understanding."
Jeremiah 3:12a-15 ESV

See, even when we as worship leaders or believers get out of place with God and we begin to do things in our own strength and/or for our own name, God still leaves room for reconciliation. For forgiveness. Then in His word He promises to give us shepherds that will love us and assist us with His heart. If you can identify with this place, I feel led to say a prayer with you and give you some keys to recovery.

- You've identified that it is you! The greatest deception is self-deception, so this is the first and hardest step.
- Repent.
- Pray the following prayer with me.

Prayer for Restoration of the Wilderness Worship Leader:

> *"Lord I recognize that I have been operating out of a place of hurt and offense with my giftings and callings. I allowed the negative and positive experiences I had to turn me away from Your church, Your body, and You. I repent for this now. I ask for Your forgiveness and I now understand the error in which I have operated in. Wash me of all unrighteousness and heal me in those broken places that have been wounded and motivated me to leave Your order. I thank You Lord for granting me access to forgiveness and the Father. Now Lord, I activate Jeremiah 3:11-15 in my life. I ask You Lord for wisdom in selecting a covering, leadership. Show me who to connect with. Show me who can embrace me and lead me and nurse me back to health. I need Your guidance. Until You lead me to that place, I submit my gifts and callings to You and I make a commitment to come under Your covering. I will not operate without Your leading and Your approval. I humble myself that Your mighty hand may be at work in my life. I'm sorry Lord and I thank You for granting me mercy and showing me Your unfailing love. I trust You!*
> *In Jesus Name,*
> *Amen.*

First, pursue relationship. It's time to deal with the cause that brought the effect. Now that you have prayed, and you have repented, released it, and activated the word, now you need to begin to build back relationship with the Father. This is such an important step. In relationship, in prayer, fasting, and alone time in His presence God will begin to reveal what wounds are present and what order He wants to address them in. He will take you through behavioral patterns and commonalities in behaviors that led to this. He will show you the lack of communication you and He had. He will show you how pride came in. He will show what relationships stroked your ego and not your spiritual stability. He will become a revealer and the intimacy between you and Him will become beautiful and strong.

Second, continue to pray for direction and seek a local body. You NEED a church home! Finally, connect, submit, learn, grow, go forth in that order.

Leading from a place outside of God's instruction and order, do not allow jealousy and pride to put you in a place of corruption with God's things. I encourage you to repent and turn, that you may be redeemed and washed clean because judgement will be brought into the body of Christ. God will be seeking answers from those in authority who mishandled the sheep.

Hindrances from seeing Glory

Repent therefore, and turn back, that your sins may be blotted out, that times of refreshing may come from the presence of the Lord.
Acts 3:19 ESV

There is a standard to carry God's glory and to experience glory. As worship leaders we should be very intentional about knowing the difference between the anointing and the glory. The glory of God is a reflection of Eden. The dwelling of His manifested presence. Perfection. Completion. Abundance.

The number one hindrance from the presence of the Lord is unconfessed sin. A life of unrepentance is a dangerous life full of manifestations of the evil one. It can allow full access to demonic forces and can begin to contaminate your spirit. Unrepented sin causes distance between you and the Father and therefore plugs up the flow of the river of His presence. Notice the scripture above again. In order to experience times of refreshing in the presence of the Lord, you must be in a place of right fellowship. God hates sin and when we as His children have tainted vessels, we cannot be used, and we cannot experience the fullness of the throne of God. I believe the reason why we do not experience great manifestations of glory in churches is because of the unconfessed sin that exists. In my experience, we are more prone to deal with the outward sin, but inward sin is where we fail to examine ourselves. God sees the heart and His standard has, is, and will always be holiness. We grade ourselves on a curve, but God grades according to His word. His standard. His truth. Do not be misled worship leader! Just because God's presence came does **NOT** mean that **YOU** are in right standing. God is faithful and in spite of us He comes to meet the needs of His people. It's amazing how our spirits can yield during worship but cannot die to ourselves and commit to a life of holiness.

The second hindrance is pride. Pride will prevent you from repenting which will cause you to not experience the fullness of God's presence. God is opposed to the proud. James 4:6 NLT states, "And he gives grace generously. *As the scriptures say, "God opposes the proud but gives grace to the humble."* He clearly states in His word that pride and arrogance is evil to Him. We can become prideful in so many ways. The best way I can define it is, "thinking more highly of yourself than you ought or too lowly of yourself than you ought". Pride is feeling like you don't need God. It is a dangerous place to be when you feel like you don't need God.

A third hindrance is lack of hunger. Hunger has a posture. It is positioned a certain way. Let me describe hunger. Have you ever seen a hungry baby? They can't even communicate verbally what they desire but their cry is so desperate that it evokes a response from the parent. The parent is struggling to figure out is it the diaper that needs to be changed, do they desire to be held, or is it that they are hungry. They examine the last time they were fed but because of the desperate cry and posture of the baby they run to meet the need and then feed them, and the baby is soothed. He is **satisfied** and **fulfilled**. So, as it is with us and our Heavenly Father. When we hunger and thirst after righteousness, we have a posture, a cry, or a position, that evokes a response from heaven and it causes the Father to fill us. But pride causes us to not desire hunger. So many believers lack hunger and therefore our posture is upright versus downright.

Upright is an independent position and downright is a dependent position. Upright shows a belief that no one else is needed - it's a confidence in self. The upright man or woman exhibits pride because they are unwilling to receive from Christ or anyone else. Downright represents the posture of a toddler or a baby… it's low and dependent. Matthew 18:4 NKJV says, *"Therefore whoever humbles himself like this child is the greatest in the kingdom of heaven."* Just as a baby recognizes their need for their parent, so should it be with us as we recognize our need for Christ.

You'd be surprised how many people in the body of Christ are riding the wave of their last meal. It digested and passed through, but they have the after taste in their mouth and can't discern that it's feeding time again. We should always remain in a posture to be poured into. Lack of hunger is like a cancer, it can spread and manifest itself in many ways. It can begin to create tumors (growth). Pride is a growth! Jealousy, comparison, and unforgiveness all of those are growths. These growths cover your passion and zeal... and your worship. Surgery is the only way that tumors can be removed. They must be cut out. Surgery only occurs in the presence of God. Therefore, repent and allow God's presence to cut out the growths that seek to cover your spiritual organs and shut down your function and hinder you carrying glory.

WHO LEADS THE WORSHIP LEADER?

Jesus Christ is the ultimate worship leader. Therefore, leading worship that does not have Jesus Christ at the center is not true worship. Bryan Chappell writes this in *Christ-Centered Worship*: "There is not worship without him. The worship leader issues God's invitation to join the heavenly throne that already and always praises Him. We do not approach God on our terms, but His. When He speaks, it is our obligation and privilege to respond appropriately in praise, prayer, repentance, testimony, encouragement of others and service to what He declares about Himself."

We corporately respond to God and His revelation. One of my mentors once said to me, "You can't take us anywhere that you haven't gone." I asked the Lord to give me a revelation on what she meant by that. I believe she told me that I have to travel to the Throne Room, so I know what route to take to get others there, and I have to know what's required to stay there. As I continue to dwell there it won't be hard to teach others on how to dwell there. The more I began to dwell the more I understood the importance of partnering with the Holy Spirit when it comes to leading worship. I'll say this, the Holy Spirit is the Spirit of truth and knows what is needed for every atmosphere and knows every person. If we as worship leaders lean on the wisdom and direction of the Holy Spirit, then find rest in knowing that nothing will ever be lacking. When you discover this truth, it alleviates the pressure from the leader. Operating under the pressure is heavy and leads to burnout, exhaustion, and frustration. You can find yourself critiquing every worship moment and wondering was it effective. People always say minister to the audience of one. I want to challenge that. Do not get me wrong, that is a true statement and is useful for aligning us with the purpose of what we do, which is to glorify God Almighty. When we are ministering, we are not just ministering to an audience of one. There's an audience of people. Lol. There is a people desiring to connect with God and to encounter the presence that they have heard about or read about in the Word of God. You cannot minister to an audience of one and it is corporate worship. Develop a mindset and heart posture that you minister as unto the Lord before the audience of many but for the approval of one, which is Jesus Christ.

Having the heart of your leaders

What can I say? My church is an apostolic prophetic house that embraces the totality of the Trinity and the gifts of the Holy Spirit. It is a house that preaches truth and encourages a personal cultivation of relationship with Christ. My local house, where I actively serve, delivered me, brought healing and awakened purpose in me. I bless God for a local house of strength, love, and challenges. I was challenged to grow there. God sent me there in 2015 and I am grateful for the growth that has been taking place in me over the last few years. I love my church because my leaders care about the condition of your soul over your giftings. They strive to equip you for Kingdom impact and not for selfish gain. They desire to see you walk in your calling that God has ordained for you. I remember when I had people inquiring about having me come and minister, I made up in my mind that I will not accept any engagement without talking to my leaders first. That's honor and order. They literally pray over me and cover me as I go out. I'm accountable to God first, and then to my leadership.

Being covered and in alignment with God's established order is so pleasing to God. Obeying this system will unlock doors for you and provide promotion. Once you get connected, you will find that knowing the heart of your leaders will help you become a better worship leader. Every ministry has a stamp that uniquely identifies who they are, even within the same denomination. There are denominations within denominations. When I connected to my local church, I had to get the DNA (doctrine of the new assignment) of that house. This should be done before you operate, if not, it can cause you to become a direct contradiction to the teachings and structure of that house. I recommend taking time to get to know the ministry's mission and vision. You should participate in many events and activities. By doing so you begin to cultivate the vision, echo the vision, and you have knowledge of what the leaders want to see for the music ministry and overall for the house. When you minister you should strive to be a reflection of the vision that has gone forth. It should always align. The music and the message are the two main components of the gathering. They have to always be saying the same thing. In Mark 3:25 NKJV Jesus says, *"And if a house is divided against itself, that house cannot stand."*

Being a worship leader and being entrusted with such an assignment is nothing to be taken lightly. You are an integral part of the progression of a ministry, so much so, that the enemy would love to corrupt your heart and mind to redirect the influence. Remember the enemy brings confusion and division, but when you echo the vision it provides a deeper unity in the house and God can propel the entire church into the next level. It will allow the church to be on an accelerated track. God will use the music ministry to be on the front lines and pave the way for the others.

That is another reason why the enemy seeks to dismantle music ministries in churches. If a local house cannot come together in unity to worship the Lord in spirit and in truth the house will remain stagnant. Why? Because in worship Gods manifested presence comes to reveal and heal. The anointing is present to remove burdens and break the yoke of bondage so that deliverance and freedom and true change takes place. The enemy seeks to steal worship because it has the ability to transform and mold us more into an image of Christ. As you're molded into an image of Christ, you gain the mind of Christ, your decisions reflect Christ and you walk in your Christ-delegated authority, you begin to carry out the commission of Christ, and it stunts the operation of Satan.

Another thing to know when knowing the heart of your leaders is being open for correction and rebuke. Remain teachable and know that with any ministry error can come. If you develop a life of humility, then correction won't bring offense and make you separate from leadership or even leading. I'll address offense a little later on. I have learned the hard way unfortunately. Here's my spiel. People always say be humble. Stay humble. Wear the cloak of humility. I never hear people say how. So, I have learned that when you recognize the Sovereignty of our God then you realize that you are who you are because of Him and not because of yourself. Remember He is the one who anoints our head with oil and not we ourselves. Apart from Him we can do nothing. That mindset brings about a right spirit and clean hands and pure heart. Reading His word and abiding in Him through prayer and worship and righteous living produces humility because you're living inside the glory realm.

SEEKING THE SOUND OF THE HOUSE

The enemy has an agenda when it comes to the local churches in the body of Christ. His main mission in a local house is to see them immobilized. The enemy forms weapons against the sound of the house. John 10:10 AMP says, "The thief only comes in order to steal and kill and destroy. I came that they may have and enjoy life, and have it in abundance [to the full, till it overflows]." That can also be stated that the thief comes in order to steal and kill and destroy worship. The enemy loves to control an atmosphere. If he can get a church to be religious and welcome a doctrine of devils and have them not worship the true and living God, then he will get glory. As a worship leader it is important to pray for your local church and also for your music ministry as they are essential in creating a sound. On the day of Pentecost, they experienced a sound when the rushing mighty wind came, and they were baptized with the Holy Spirit. When the Day of Pentecost had fully come, they were all with one accord in one place.

And suddenly there came a sound from heaven, as of a rushing mighty wind, and it filled the whole house where they were sitting." Acts 2:1-2 NKJV

Seeking the sound of the house requires intentional prayer and study where you ask God to reveal what is needed for the house that you serve in or minister to. You can ask God to place a spirit of Issachar on you to be able to sense the seasons and times that the house is in. The sons of Issachar were known for their wisdom and had understanding of the timing of God. 1 Chronicles mentions the sons of Issachar briefly stating, *"From the tribe of Issachar, there were 200 leaders of the tribe with their relatives. All these men understood the signs of the times and knew the best course for Israel to take." 1 Chronicles 12:32 NKJV* That is so powerful! What would happen if we fully understood what God was doing and where He was moving at any given time? Well, there is good news… we can! We have access not only to our Heavenly Father but to His will and His plan. If you seek Him, then He will reveal exactly the place or season a ministry is in, thus also unveiling the sound that is needed in that hour. Understanding the sound that is needed to be released in a house (ministry) is vital to proper selection of song selection and ministering as a whole. You should constantly be asking yourself what is God saying for the church?

Fasting for Power in Worship

Fasting according to the Webster Dictionary is a willing abstinence or reduction from some food, drink, or both, for a period of time. Fasting for the believer is such a powerful tool. Fasting is exchanging physical pleasures for God. True fasting brings a realignment. It gets God involved in our lives. According to Isaiah 58, fasting can undo the bonds of wickedness and tear to pieces the ropes of the yoke. It lets the oppressed go free and breaks yokes. True fasting involves not only the absence of food but also the presence of prayer. If you are not praying while fasting, then you are only abstaining and NOT fasting. In giving you the backdrop for fasting it is important to know how this applies to the worship leader. As a leader your job is to usher people into the presence of God and when you lack power and authority or anointing you should consider a fast. Fasting is a sure way to bask in the glory of God. When you sacrifice yourself for intimate time with the Father He rewards with glory. Hebrews 11:6 NKJV says, "But without faith it is impossible to please Him, for he who comes to God must believe that He is, and that He is a rewarder of those who diligently seek Him." When you seek Him, He rewards with attributes of Himself. Glory is in the makeup of the Father. He gives it to us. It's a manifestation of Him!

> *I have given them the glory you gave me, so they may be one as we are one. - John 17:22 NLT*

It connects you to the Father on a deeper level! It will allow you to be more in tune with the spiritual realm. Most definitely.

> *Is this not the type of fasting I have chosen: to loose the bonds of wickedness, to undo the heavy burdens, to let the oppressed go free, and that you break every yoke?*
> *Isaiah 58:6-7 NKJV*

Based on that scripture, fasting produces four things.

- Looses the bonds of wickedness
- Undoes the heavy burdens
- The oppressed go free
- Broken yokes

Personal fasting causes a shift in your natural man because it is now denied and coming into the obedience of Christ. It is a powerful and effective tool to incorporate into your walk with Christ. Whatever area you are struggling in, fasting will help you identify the root and deal with it accordingly. You'll have keen insight on what steps should be taken to gain back power and control over yourself. There is also another layer of fasting where you have specific objectives before the Lord to accomplish. If you desire unity within your local house, or for a freedom in worship like you've never experienced, then I encourage you to fast for it. If you want to see it manifested then push back your plate, put down the remote control, get off social media and fervently seek for the purpose to be fulfilled. When you fast, there is a freedom and victory anointing that will rest on you for ministering. It rests on you to *do*! To accomplish!

Fasting for power in worship also aides you for the amount of warfare that takes place during a corporate worship setting. There are wicked forces that seek to hinder or eliminate the move of God. For the worship leader fasting produces power and the power comes to demonstrate. The anointing that flows allows people's lives to be changed beyond the worship set and beyond Sunday morning. It removes the power of darkness from them that they may experience a liberty in Christ Jesus. That explains why the enemy is so against the believer fasting, and also why there is so much resistance in atmospheres week after week in church. When there is a free flow then the work of the Holy Spirit takes control and people begin to put sin down and be transformed by His spirit. So, having been consecrated before the Father you have power in your spirit man to withstand the battles that occur in any atmosphere. The enemy knows that when you truly walk in the boldness and authority you've been given by Jesus Christ that he is defeated. Walk in your authority!

Look, I have given you authority over all the power of the enemy, and you can walk among snakes and scorpions and crush them. Nothing will injure you.
Luke 10:19 NLT

Heart Check

Worship also exposes your heart. If it is damaged, broken or contaminated it will flow out of you. The enemy seeks to corrupt our hearts because it hurts our witness. It hinders our effectiveness for God. When we as worship leaders do not consistently assess our hearts then those insecurities, rejection, offense, bitterness, shame, and pride will be on display before the people. It is important that worship leaders go through seasons of deliverance and seek after maturity to develop in areas that are needed. Now there will be times God will use that vulnerable space to relate to His people and draw them in. But be advised, it is Spirit-led not emotion-led. You have to know and learn the difference. We just need to be available. John 12:32 NKJV says, "And I, if I am lifted up from the earth, will draw all peoples to Myself." We just have to do the lifting and then He heals, sets free, comforts, delivers, blesses, gives answers, grants peace, provides joy, which builds up our strength, gives strategy and clarity. I have found that worship leaders still feel unworthy to lift Him up. We allow doubt, fear, insecurity, and sin to become the very thing that sews the veil back up instead of us realizing that we have access because of Jesus Christ's sacrifice. His grace is sufficient, and He is just to forgive us. Do not allow the past to become the blockage week after week that makes you guarded in His presence. How can you sing a song that pleads for you to be vulnerable in His presence and that His presence is transformational, but you are still unable to be that in and of yourself?

What is Availability?

I find myself asking this question a lot. Lord what does it mean to be available to you? It simply means to be surrendered and obedient. Isaiah 1:19 NIV says, *"If you are willing and obedient, you will eat the good things of the land."* We can be surrendered but not obedient. What would it benefit a congregation if your worship was pure, but you failed in obedience to release something, or to be quiet, or to sing a specific song to shift an atmosphere? I promise people take this assignment for granted. I did not know much about warfare and spirits until God gave me a platform to make His name great through worship leading. When I would step on the stage it was like God gave me a spiritual insight and I could begin to sense everything in the spiritual realm. But, the enemy got me to fall as it relates to obedience. It happens more than people want to admit.

> *Your anointing is not a substitution for your obedience.*
> *God can see past your mask.*

Musicians experience this too. They are so technical and put so much emphasis on the structure or pattern of the song and the sound, or the run or riff that we forget that even in a worship service it's a matter of life and death. Don't seek the anointing more than you seek God. We cannot allow our programs to interfere with our obedience. We must submit and be in order and have complete obedience. At my home church, my leaders teach us that the worship team is of as much importance as the preached word of God. It makes the heart pliable and ready to receive from God. In my opinion, it is of greater importance than we actually can comprehend because the Word teaches you the principles to navigate through life and presents revelation to what God meant in His written word but in worship it can be God's spoken word and manifested presence that can change your life. In an evident, tangible atmosphere, God can do everything He needs to do, and your life can be forever changed.

God also gave me a revelation of availability. He explained to me why I couldn't be used. I am 100% sure it applies to us all. In my office I have a dry erase board and one day the Lord instructed me to write the scripture that says, "Create in me a clean heart and renew a right spirit within me." Psalm 51:10 KJV. He then said, "place a parenthesis behind the word right, and write in holy, pure, loving and then close the parenthesis." So, I read the scripture like this, *"Create in me a clean heart and renew a right (holy, pure, loving) spirit within me!"* I didn't think anything of it until the next day when I entered my office to start my work day. I sat down, and the Holy Spirit said, "look at the board." The Holy Spirit asked me a question. You know when you're asked a question by the one that carries all wisdom, it's for you and not the Holy Spirit. Lol. He asked, "Sarenina do you know that you can have a clean heart and not a right spirit?" I blinked twice to look at it to get a better understanding and then He illuminated it to me. It was like the words and meaning jumped off the board and into my heart. My spirit leaped! I was stunned! I could not believe it. He said, "you need both! A clean heart AND a right spirit." I then asked, "what is a right spirit?"

He responded with "I told you. Look at the scripture."

Behold, there it was, right (holy, pure, loving). The Holy Spirit is so amazing in how He communicates with me. We know God speaks to us through His written word, visions, dreams, someone else, prophecy, nature, and/or spontaneous thoughts. He showed me a vision of my prayers and how they were directed to having a clean heart, but I didn't put emphasis on possessing a right spirit. I was taught that you can do a right thing with a wrong spirit but that day I LEARNED you can do something with a good motive and clean heart but not the right spirit. As a worship leader it is imperative to strive to possess BOTH. You also need to learn how the Holy Spirit speaks to you. If you haven't solidified how God communicates to you then how can you be certain that it is indeed Him speaking and not the enemy, or your own thoughts. I don't think you can be certain. Let's fix that!

Hearing the Voice of God

Hearing the voice of God is not only imperative for every believer, but it is equally important, if not more, for the worship leader. When leading worship, we are first and foremost sons and daughters of the most High God. I'll discuss sonship later in this chapter. It is Christ who is the true worship leader. But how can we truly follow Him and lead others if we don't know His voice?

In our leading of worship, we are keeping it Christ-centered and creating an atmosphere for His agenda to be fulfilled. It isn't about us. It is exactly what Jesus said when He spoke about His Father (God) in John 8,

"... But the One who sent Me is truthful, and what I have heard from Him, I tell the world." (verse 26) and *"... then you will understand that I am He. I do nothing on my own but say only what the Father taught me."* (verse 28). So, then we should seek to have this same posture. We 'say' and 'sing' only what God speaks. But in order to do that we have to know His voice. In order to know the voice of the Lord *we have to know His word and spend time in His presence. John 1:1 NIV says "In the beginning was the Word, and the Word was with God, and the Word was God." So, we learn who God is and how He speaks by studying His word.*

For now, let's look at an example in the word of God of someone who had to learn how to hear the voice of God for himself. Samuel was a young boy when his parents dedicated him back to God because God answered Hannah's petition for a son. He lived in the temple of the Lord, located in Shiloh, and was raised by the priest Eli (see 1 Samuel 1 - 2). Samuel was young, nevertheless, he assisted Eli the priest and served the Lord.

Meanwhile, the boy Samuel served the Lord by assisting Eli. Now in those days messages from the Lord were very rare, and visions were quite uncommon. One night Eli, who was almost blind by now, had gone to bed. The lamp of God had not yet gone out, and Samuel was sleeping in the Tabernacle near the Ark of God. Suddenly the Lord called out, "Samuel!" "Yes?" Samuel replied. "What is it?" He got up and ran to Eli. "Here I am. Did you call me?" "I didn't call you," Eli replied. "Go back to bed." So he did. Then the Lord called out again, "Samuel!"

Again, Samuel got up and went to Eli. "Here I am. Did you call me?" "I didn't call you, my son," Eli said. "Go back to bed." Samuel did not yet know the Lord because he had never had a message from the Lord before. So, the Lord called a third time, and once more Samuel got up and went to Eli. "Here I am. Did you call me?" Then Eli realized it was the Lord who was calling the boy. So, he said to Samuel, "Go and lie down again, and if someone calls again, say, 'Speak, Lord, your servant is listening.'" So Samuel went back to bed. And the Lord came and called as before, "Samuel! Samuel!" And Samuel replied, "Speak, your servant is listening." (1 Samuel 3:1 - 10 NLT)

We can learn several things from Samuel when it comes to developing our ear to hear God's voice.

Samuel stayed in the presence of the Lord. The word of God says "...Meanwhile, Samuel grew up in the presence of the Lord." 1 Samuel 2:21 NLT One may say that Samuel was automatically set to hear God because he dwelled in the temple. But this isn't true as we can look at Eli's sons, Hophni and Phinehas, who were operating as priests for the Lord but had no respect for God. 1 Samuel 2:12 NLT states, *"Now the sons of Eli were scoundrels who had no respect for the Lord."* So, it is possible to grow up in the presence of God and go "through the motions" of serving Him, but not have any reverence for the Lord. Samuel was different even though he received the same training and development as Eli's sons. Moreover, Eli had reached an old age by the time he began raising Samuel, which some may see as a disadvantage for Samuel. However, God was raising up Samuel to be a man who would serve the Lord all the days of his life. So, Samuel stayed in God's presence and he created an atmosphere conducive for God to dwell in. Let me ask you, what kind of environment have you created for God to abide in?

Samuel made a choice to serve and honor the Lord. As stated in the aforementioned, Eli's sons were wicked and did evil in the temple of the Lord. Although they were raised in the temple and received the same training as Samuel, they chose to manipulate God's people and mistreat the Lord's sacrifice. (1 Samuel 2:12 - 17 NLT) However, Samuel made a decision to serve the Lord. So, it is the same with us. We can grow up in church all our lives and still be far away from God. If we aren't careful, our worship will become tainted and we will no longer be able to hear or discern the voice of God. If you want to hear the voice of God, you must make a conscious decision to serve and honor the Lord. When we reverence the Lord with honor and servitude, then we are positioning our hearts to hear from Him. How do you intentionally honor God in your life?

Samuel gave God permission and/ or access to speak to him. After the third time that Samuel ran to Eli, Eli gave the young boy clear instructions. Eli said, "Then Eli realized it was the Lord who was calling the boy. So he said to Samuel, "Go and lie down again, and if someone calls again, say, 'Speak, Lord, your servant is listening.'" So Samuel went back to bed. And the Lord came and called as before, "Samuel! Samuel!" And Samuel replied, "Speak, your servant is listening." Samuel heard the voice of

God all the times before when he mistakenly thought it was Eli. However, he had to acknowledge the Lord in order to be in a position to hear all of what God was saying.

Samuel's response each time he heard God's voice was a posture of obedience. When we hear the voice of the Lord, we have to be willing to walk in obedience or we won't go far. Obedience unlocks the blessings of the Lord, but it also keeps us in the right posture before the Lord. Can you imagine your parent calling your name in the middle of the night while you are asleep? Then in response to hearing your name, you have to get up and go to their room to see what they needed. Every single time. Well imagine what it was like for Samuel this particular night. Samuel was asleep and three distinct times he heard his name and "ran" to Eli. He didn't say "never mind" or "I'll check in the morning". No, Samuel's response each time he heard his name called was to get up and see what was requested of him. We should seek to have this same response each time we hear the voice of the Lord. The truth is, it's an honor to have our names called by God and for Him to choose to speak to us. Perhaps if we truly reverenced the voice of God as the children of Israel did in the Old Testament, we would be in a better position to hear God's voice without interference. No matter how comfortable we are, we need to be ready to "run" when God speaks. No matter how conditioned we are, we have to be willing to "get up" every single time God calls our name. No matter how consumed we are with our own wants and desires, we have to be ready to "answer" with obedience every single time God says our name. Every single time.

Samuel submitted to Godly leadership. This point goes hand in hand with point #4. Samuel was submitted to Eli's leadership and respected him. Each time Samuel thought Eli called him, he ran to him without hesitation. Keep in mind, this was in the middle of the night and surely Samuel desired to fully rest. But that didn't stop him from being obedient. As a matter of fact, he had such a respect for the priest of the Lord (Eli) that he got up three different times to respond to the call. I believe that if Eli hadn't provided clear instructions on the third time that Samuel would have continued to rise and go to Eli's side. Who are you submitted to in your local house? Who feeds you spiritually and nurtures your desire to hear from God? This is important to ask and reflect on because oftentimes we learn how to hear God's voice from the leadership we submit to. You can ask the question of what would have happened if Eli wasn't present to give guidance and instruction? I believe God would have still used Samuel, but his training may have taken longer. It would have also given way to Samuel being confused or frustrated in his process more than necessary.

Who we are submitted to, matters. Even though Eli didn't correct or intervene with his son's and their wicked exploits, he still had a reverence for the Lord. This is evident when Samuel gives him an unfavorable word from the Lord and Eli's response is essentially "let God's will be done". In 1 Samuel 3:18 NLT it says, *"So Samuel told Eli everything; he didn't hold anything back. "It is the Lord's will," Eli replied. "Let him do what he thinks best."* The Lord just pronounced judgement on Eli and his entire family and Eli's response still showed reverence to God. We can learn so much from the leadership in our local church. The questions remain, are we connected to the right leadership, are we listening, and do we have a heart to hear?

So, we can see through dissecting Samuel's early life, that hearing God's voice comes with a responsibility. It is imperative that every believer, but definitely every worship leader, know the voice of the Lord. Furthermore, for the worship leader it isn't good enough to hear the voice of God, but we have a mandate to obey the voice of the Lord. This means every time we lead the people of God into the presence of the Lord we have to be connected and intentional about following the unction of the Holy Spirit. We don't call the shots, the Holy Spirit does. When He moves, we ought to follow. When the Holy Spirit gives the next step, we have an obligation to the Lord and the people we lead to obey. After all, in the presence of the true and living God there are no titles. When we stand before the One True King, we are standing as sons and daughters. It is our sonship given to us when we accepted Christ as our savior and our obedience that really matters in His presence.

Accountability for Sonship

Remember that you can't get so distracted with serving that you forget about your sonship. The Word of God states that we are sons of God. Matthew 5:9 NKJV states, *"Blessed are the peacemakers, For they shall be called sons of God."* We are disciples first. So, it is important to receive the word, study, and learn. As a believer you should be a forever learner. Leaders still have a responsibility to work out their salvation with fear and trembling not with entitlement and arrogance.

> *Therefore, my beloved as you have always obeyed, not as in my presence only, but now much more in my absence, work out your own salvation with fear and trembling; for it is God who works in you both to will and to do for His good pleasure.*
> *Philippians 2:12 NKJV*

Leaders are not above the principles God set in place. We are to follow them even the more. We are to be humble, keep a servant's heart at all times, watch pride and the spirit of competition. Stay Kingdom focused, and it will always be known to you that your position is for people. Never for you!

That is why having accountability is beneficial to worship leaders. There is such a demand on needing to know what the Lord is speaking, so it helps to have people cover you. You have to be covered in every area of your life. Being covered to me means you must become naked and allow someone to provide the clothes. That is good to me. See, if you are not willing to get undressed how can someone come and bathe you (cleanse you with the word of God and clothe you with wisdom and principle and swaddle you in prayer and intercession). A major factor of my ministry involves having spiritual parents that nourish me, bathe me, and correct me. That also means that they can hurt my feelings and still love me, then prepare me, warn me, then celebrate me, then cry, hurt with me, and then educate me. It's a beautiful thing! Where can I go as a vessel of God if I don't allow the people God placed in my life to operate in their assignment, which is me.

We are assigned to people and people are assigned to us. Think about Ruth and Naomi. How could Ruth enter into her new destiny unless her obedient heart aligned with what God was doing? Sometimes we allow familiarity and position to overrule the purpose of the connection. Don't get caught up that you miss the impartation because you feel that a close friend or family member, or church member couldn't possibly give you what you need. How arrogant? So, God can't use them? The influence they have in your life should benefit your spiritual and personal development and growth. If not, then it isn't Kingdom. God strategically placed people in my life to mother and father me; it forced me to grow up quickly. I am still growing. As long as you're breathing you need people in place. The day I say to myself I no longer need accountability is the day God sits my prideful self-down and calls me home.

The Gift of the Holy Spirit

The gift of the Holy Spirit is a game-changer for the believer. It allows you to come into an awareness and intimacy with God like you cannot imagine. Many are aware of God the Father because He is Almighty and Creator of heaven and earth, and then through God the Son we receive salvation and are reconciled back to God the Father, but many have not encountered God, the Holy Spirit. The Holy Spirit is a person who Jesus gave to us as a Helper and a Guide. He is the Spirit of truth. He leads, instructs, and enables us to walk according to the laws that God the Father set in place. He is Jesus' Spirit. We need Him! Many worship leaders come from so many teachings that do not recognize the power and beauty of the Holy Spirit. They are afraid of the Holy Spirit because He has been portrayed as spooky or weird. In reality, the Holy Spirit is the One who gives us power to do the work of the ministry. He assists us in carrying out the mandate of God the Father and God the Son. Being filled with the Holy Spirit with the evidence of speaking in tongues is so beautiful. Here are some of the benefits:

- ❖ Wisdom/Insight
- ❖ Comfort
- ❖ Operation in the Gifts of the Holy Spirit
- ❖ Songs and Thanksgiving
- ❖ Unhindered prayers

Being a worship leader, God can also allow you to be activated and operate in the gifts of the Holy Spirit. We need the gifts of the Holy Spirit and the fruit of the Holy Spirit. Demonstrations should always follow God's chosen. His anointing should always follow God's chosen. It displays that God is working and moving. The anointing upon you is for service. It is for operation. Whether it be prophetic worship or an utterance, word of knowledge and word of wisdom, gift of prophecy, healing, and my favorite, gift of tongues they should all flow out of the worship leader. It is for the edification of the Church.

Most worship leaders think they do not need the baptism of the Holy Spirit with the evidence of unknown tongues because they feel as if they are already effective without it. They could have also received wrong teachings and be connected to a local church that ignores the entire book of Acts. I have also been in Christian settings where it was stated that "we are already filled with the Holy Spirit, so we don't need it." When we are born again, we are filled with God's spirit and He dwells on the inside of us but then there is another baptism that comes to give you power. According to Matthew 3:11 NLT, John states: *"I baptize with water those who repent of their sins and turn to God. But someone is coming soon who is greater than I am-so much greater that I'm not worthy even to be his slave and carry his sandals. He will baptize you with the Holy Spirit and with fire."*

I would say that as a worship leader it is indescribable what being baptized in the Holy Spirit does for you. Songs just pour out from you. Spontaneously and prophetically. You have a direct line to the one who knows all, so now there is a great well of wisdom that you have access to as well. Jesus understood the magnitude of the Holy Spirit, which is why He instructed the disciples not to leave until they received it. They could not fulfill the mandate without having Him. If you are not baptized in the Holy Spirit with the evidence of speaking in tongues pray the following prayer:

Prayer for Speaking in Tongues

Heavenly Father, I come in the name of Jesus Christ and I desire the baptism of the Holy Spirit with the evidence of speaking in tongues. Please forgive me for any of my sins and any unforgiveness I may have, I release it right now in Jesus' name. Your word says that the gift of the Holy Spirit comforts us and guides us. He also gives us access to other gifts of the Spirit and we have access to God's power to walk out the assignment and mandate on our life. I want the kind of power to do Your will Lord. I know that the receiving of this gift is supernatural and a miracle because it surpasses all human reasoning. Your word says that I can have it, and I receive this gift by faith in the name of Jesus. Baptize me with Your fire! I know my life will never be the same. I thank you for Your baptism and help me to continue living for You. May this fire never burn out and always keep me close to You. I love you Lord and thank You for this new heavenly language and for the gift of the Holy Spirit.

In Jesus' name, Amen.

PROPHETIC WORSHIP LEADERS

What is needed for the now? What is God saying today and for the gathering of people? Worship leaders should desire the prophetic because that is where rhema words come from. Being activated in the prophetic does not mean you are called by God to be a prophet. Jesus gave gifts unto men, but He **assigned** offices as He saw fit in the earth. It does not mean you have to always speak or sing a prophetic word. You can prophesy with the right song choice. You can prophesy with the right gesture or the right exhortation. Spending quality time in prayer and worship, and learning to discern the voice of God helps us to be sensitive or sharpened to know what God is saying in that hour, or in that worship moment. Worship moments happen so quickly. What is the Lord saying? What does He want to do? If you don't know, how can you lead. Sometimes we can be activated and still not know. How to hear the voice of God aids your worship leading. What are the proper songs? How to hear if there is a shift that needs to happen in the atmosphere, and how to properly sense that. God's heart is souls! He wants his creation reconciled back to Him. He wants lives to be changed. He desires that none perish but that all may come to know Him. He wants people to be drawn to Him. He wants to do the drawing. 1 Corinthians 14:1 NIV says, "Follow the way of love and eagerly desire gifts of the Spirit, especially prophecy. Worship leaders should be activated and have an awareness of the gifts of the Holy Spirit. Every believer has the ability to prophesy. (1 Corinthians 14:31) If you are not activated in the prophetic and desire to be, then get with the Prophet appointed by leadership to your church, begin to study and learn about the prophetic. Once you are activated it is time to practice and build yourself in the area of leading prophetically.

Without the element of the prophetic you are only scratching the surface as a worship leader. Break the glass ceiling of what is currently defined as worship leading. Activation in the prophetic takes you to a whole new level in relationship, anointing, and war! I will break those 3 things down.

Relationship

Exploring the prophetic opens up a new layer in your relationship with the Lord. When you begin to seek after the prophetic you give the Lord access to deeper parts of you spiritually. You develop a sensitivity to the voice of the Lord and you lean on His leading. There is also another layer of obedience that is required for flowing in the prophetic. In order for God to truly use you, He will need to purify the vessel in which His voice or song flows through. Deliverance and Purging will follow. God will never allow purity to flow through an impure vessel. This is different from the gift of prophecy. Romans 11:29 KJV says, *"For the gifts and calling of God are without repentance."* So, you can deliver a word of prophecy to someone and not be a pure vessel, but in order to carry the mantle of prophetic worship you will need to be purified. Dictionary.com defines purify as a verb to make pure; free from anything that debases, pollutes, adulterates, or contaminates. There is a myth that people can achieve this level of operation without any requirement from them. That is false. God will require more from you. You will have to be free from anything that contaminates you as the vessel. You cannot actively participate in sin or serve idols and think that your anointing will carry you over and that God does not see you. Proverbs 5:21 NLT says, *"For the Lord sees clearly what a man does, examining every path he takes."* Saul was under the same impression when he was commanded by God to kill everything. God fired him even though he was still "king" to the people. Meaning you can still be leading worship every Sunday, but God's hand is no longer on you. The oil (anointing) has left the building. God will not be mocked!

Prophetic worship is more than edification, exhortation and comfort, it is designed to do. It comes to manifest the presence of God in a way to produce something, whether that be miracles, healings, deliverance, repentance, praise, or a specific response for a specific outcome. What I have found in flowing as a prophetic worshiper is that when God sings through me, or allows me to see a vision, and instructs me to sing what I see, it is designed for a specific response for a specific outcome. He will often say, "Healing needs to take place! Sing healing!" I will listen to the spirit of the Lord and sing what He's saying to me, and it breaks an atmosphere and allows a healing oil to flow. He could say breakthrough is needed in the house or even encouragement. He will then instruct me on what to say and the response will cause the heavens to open and for the very specific outcome to manifest. It is amazing. Flowing in the prophetic allows you to truly connect with the Lord intimately and learn His character and His heart. Get ready to spend more time in prayer, reading the Word of God and also in worship.

Record everything and journal frequently because there will be several things spoken, or sung out privately, that God will use publicly.

Anointing

Flowing in the prophetic requires a special anointing to come upon you. Due to the result being different in prophetic worship, you will find a different and unique operation and anointing that will flow out of you when prophetically worshiping. Judy Jacobs states in *You Are Anointed for This,* "The anointing that comes upon you is not your anointing. It is God's anointing, the anointing of the Holy Spirit. God is the one who gives His anointing to us. It is a free gift that comes directly from Him, and once given, it is to be shared with others. The anointing belongs to God. God's anointing releases healings, deliverances, miracles, signs, and wonders. But this same anointing also helps you live out your everyday life as one of the called-out, chosen, and appointed people of God. What is the anointing? It is joy, passion, power, glory, confidence, boldness, and authority. It makes you cry. It makes you laugh. It gives you righteous indignation. It is the power to preach, sing, witness, testify, and do spiritual warfare. It is peace. It comes suddenly, and it takes time. It is meek, and it is strong. The anointing is simply the fuel of God's presence on one for the purpose of the establishment of God's Kingdom."

War

You cannot experience the prophetic and not brace yourself for war. Remember we have a real enemy who is a thief and seeks to steal, to kill and to destroy the prophetic. He would love to consume you with thoughts of unbelief and fear to muzzle your mouth that you do not speak or sing what thus says the Lord. Understand that as long as the people remain unaware of what the Lord is saying that they will perish. When you allow the Holy Spirit to flow prophetically through you, the vessel, it brings enlightenment, direction, encouragement and victory to the people of God. With every moment of obedience there will be spiritual opposition that will come against you. Particularly in this area I would find myself discouraged and often defeated because I never could understand why I would have these amazing worship moments and God would be glorified and people would be blessed, but then for the next 7 days I would intensely be beaten spiritually. Everything would come against me. My job, family and friends. Stuff would just break out. The Holy Spirit spoke to me and said, "I need to teach your hands to war." That struck me inside. The enemy wanted me to shut my mouth and halt my impact. He would bring an onslaught of attacks against me to weigh me down and have me weary to the point of no desire of the Holy Spirit flowing freely. The devil is a liar! I learned that war is associated with this prophetic flow. If you're a worship leader and have not entered into a place of intense battle, then you simply cannot relate. How else can you explain feeling fine before service but as soon as you get ready to sing, now you have a headache. As soon as you get off the platform you are bombarded with thoughts of self-doubt and insecurity. That is why we have to allow the Holy Spirit to deal with those insecurities. Anything that the enemy can use against you, deal with it in the spirit so that he has no access points. Sometimes we can be deceived thinking that we do not have to do what everyone does because we are in leadership. I would argue that we need it more than anyone because we ARE in leadership. Do not neglect your development and process of purity. That could be the very thing that the enemy uses to attack you. Actively and aggressively deal with those areas of insecurity and fear or they will deal with you.

SELF-CARE

Due to this sense of pressure and expectation to serve, to be, and to produce, sometimes, well most times, we are not intentional with our self-care. There is a natural and spiritual aspect of self-care to consider as worship leaders. As a frequent pourer, you have to allow space to be poured in to. Even though you minster, you need to be sure to actually allot times where you are receiving the word and communing in God's presence. If you serve in a ministry where you have to minister weekly be sure to purchase the CD's/DVD's or review the sermons later. Schedule a time of personal Bible study where you can go back and eat off the message. You need to be spiritually fed.

Having the spiritual leadership pray for you and cover you is amazing, but that does not deviate from the personal development in your relationship with Christ. Make sure praying, reading the Word of God, and fasting are a part of your routine. This will keep you at the Father's feet and allow you to be refreshed consistently because you dwell in God's presence privately.

Do not forsake building an intimate relationship. My viewpoint is that when you enter into a leadership position or begin operating in any capacity in the kingdom of God you need to be in God's presence more than before. Learn how to prioritize that time you have with Jesus. Also, be sure to have proper mentorship and accountability that you can trust, and that will always make sure you are not placing your gifts in operation over your position as a son of God. I cannot begin to express how allowing your vessel to be tended to, benefits your operation as a worship leader. It breaks my heart when people who are called to worship leadership jump to be impactful but are not effective because they have not learned the process of dealing with *self*.

We are not intentional with being connected to the vine and drinking from the well constantly. We ride on our last filling and we do not keep ourselves stirred. We lack accountability. We lack mentorship. We lack healthy coping mechanisms. We get in a place of isolation. Pride. We lack in our intimate relationship with Christ. So, the enemy attacks the mind. The main thing he wants to do with a worship leader is taint the vessel and get you to shut your mouth, especially if you're a prophetic worship leader. A Psalmist is just like a prophet. So, if you're not praying, if you are not reading your word, not decreeing, not declaring, not even worshipping in your own time; then you're dry.

People minister in a dry place or dry season, and I like to call that ministering out of the reserve. Instead of ministering out of your overflow you minister out of your reserve. The reserve is designed to minister to you and the overflow is designed to minister to others. "Fill me up till I overflow." We sing the part that says I want to run over. Why is that? Because when you run over people can drink from the running over and it nourishes them but won't deplete you. That's why as worship leaders we should be constantly seeking to be filled to overflow because it is essential for effective ministry. For example, think of a budget where you have savings (reserve). Your reserve or portion sustains you. Through your overflow you can minister to the people. You have a season where you get a promotion, or you have an additional stream of income. You have more. You decide to shop and you're in a position to do it. But then when you run out, you go and dip in your savings.

One of the things worship leaders need is spiritual awareness. This awareness comes from the Holy Spirit and will show you your condition. That comes from a strong foundation in personal relationship. How many times can you say you've deadened that voice that comes to you as a warning?

Another way to receive spiritual care is to incorporate monthly meetings with your spiritual leadership. Check-ins are great for a worship leader because you are able to hear feedback on what your leaders think about how you are developing personally and spiritually. I never feel like "I've arrived, or I have nothing that needs to be changed!" That mindset can be one of great danger. Be sure to always ask questions, like how can you improve and what areas do they see that you need to mature in? Those times can be ones of refreshing for you and provide healing and/or deliverance depending on where you are. The Lord can use them to bring confirmation on what He has already shared with you, or to challenge you on something completely new that you may have not seen yet. Remember we can grade ourselves on a curve. Never allow fear to keep you from seeking spiritual self-care. God wants us to be matured in every area of our lives.

Keeping your fire kindled and your hunger as a worship leader can be the difference between you being spiritually healthy and spiritually damaging. There will be times when you feel like you are in a dry place, or a dry season. We all experience it. Two things come to mind: lack of hunger and loss of passion. When we do not realize it, we can find ourselves becoming complacent and casual with God's manifested presence. His signs and wonders do not move us like in the beginning.

We have an expectation of the oil to flow but we do not treasure the Giver of oil. We could experience intense personal and spiritual warfare that causes us to unknowingly retreat. We could easily be overwhelmed and weighed down and walk away from that private time of refreshing in God's presence, but not understanding that our hunger is not where it used to be. I encourage you to not be discouraged and walk in condemnation. Every believer can say at one time or another they have been in that place...more than once. REACH OUT! Speak up! Do not try to act like you are invisible. People see you and God knows you.

When I found myself in a dry place it baffled me because I was leading worship weekly and the oil was flowing. I was operating in my gifts and lives were being impacted for God, but I was depleted of resource. I was in the negative. We are under the illusion that because God uses us mightily that we are okay in His book. No, I am sorry that is not the case. What woke me up when I had lost my passion and hunger was when I was sitting in my car one day looking at old videos. I ran across an old worship video and I felt led to view the entire video. As I watched the video, I saw a fiery ignited woman of God ministering prophetically and the presence emanated from the video. I sat in tears thinking, "Who is that and where did she go? What happened?" The Holy Spirit interjected my thoughts and said "You left me. I miss you. Come back." Once I heard that, it was as if the Holy Spirit had re-baptized me with fire. I began to pray in my heavenly language and repent. I began to cry out for His presence and for fire. I was able to rekindle the fire inside of me. Hear me out though…I also told my mentors about this.

To encounter things in secret keeps you hidden, and the enemy can still have access, but when you get a revelation, exposing yourself can uncover the enemy and lead to freedom and victory, you will always want to share things. My mentor reminds me often to stay in God's presence. When I dwell in the glory nothing can harm me. Some indicators that you need some attention to self are; you are having little to no prayer time, not reading the Word of God, too busy to fast, and not dwelling in the secret place. If you find yourself only spending time in God's presence to receive downloads, new songs, and/or to ask Him to help you minster, then you may want to consider that you are not tending to your personal development. You can go to God to receive a download but not to receive Him. Praying for the pour with no interest in the Pourer is a clear indicator of lack of relationship with Jesus Christ. If you are in that place right now, repent and begin to remember the beauty of God and why you serve Him and who He is to you. Fall in love with Jesus all over again and keep your fire kindled.

Learn the power of NO!

Utilizing wisdom as a worship leader is extremely important. The Word of God says in James 1:5, "If any of you lacks wisdom, let him ask of God, who gives to all liberally and without reproach, and it will be given to him." That lets me know and should make you realize how God views wisdom. We need it in order to make good decisions. Wisdom is knowing what to do, when to do, and how to do. Wisdom keeps you safe. As a leader it is important to lean on the wisdom of God when it comes to knowing when to minister, what ministry engagement to accept, when you need training and when you need rest. It is so easy to become overwhelmed or depleted when leading others.

Sometimes you may have to say no. It is okay to say no. It is okay to take a break. It is okay to need to take a vacation. It is okay to not be the guest psalmist for every event. We are not like our Heavenly Father. He does not sleep but we should. He does not need rest, but He encourages us to receive that. Rest is so important to the Lord. He desires for us to have it. Rest is not just defined as physically sleeping but it is also resting in the Lord. As people of God we should always seek to achieve balance. What am I saying? Get a life! Live! Explore hobbies, travel, go forth in purpose, write a book, invest in your family, laugh, and enjoy life.

> *The Lord is my shepherd; I have all that I need. He lets me rest in green meadows; he leads me beside peaceful streams. He renews my strength...*
> *Psalm 23:1-3 NLT*

WORSHIP LEADERSHIP

LEADING A CONGREGATION

I'm there and they are not! You have to understand that everyone is at a different level spiritually. I think a great opening statement is that you as a worship leader in the local house should never be somewhere that your leadership is not or hasn't revealed that you should be. You can never see above your leadership. I think that myth should be debunked for all the super spiritual people that think they have more insight than the visionaries of the house God established. You're wrong and out of order.

The vision comes from God and is given to the senior leadership for the house. You don't know vision until the visionaries open their mouths. Do not allow a spirit of Jezebel or Ahab to creep in on this matter. Quickest way to get out of alignment is to dishonor and walk in disobedience. Just ask Saul. When leading a congregation rely on the Holy Spirit. The Holy Spirit is the all-knowing one. He is the one that in His infinite wisdom gives strategy on how to reach the congregation. So, me as a leader, when I think about leading a congregation one main thing, I think about is song selection. Song selection is extremely important. But I don't think we should be caught up in a song. The right song can minister, if the song is biblical then any song should be able to minster. Know that every song you enjoy listening to is not meant for the congregation and rightfully so. Songs should be purposeful and lead you to the Father.

As a leader you desire to choose music that's congregation engagement friendly. You want them to be engaged. You want it to be something they can sing along to, that they can connect with, that they either heard, or that has powerful biblical content that they can easily grasp and apply. That's why worship leaders should be activated and seek the sound of the house. You have to know what the house needs to hear in that particular season or particular service. Because God may be saying, "It's a new season! Behold I shall do a new thing!" but you start singing I'm trading my sorrows by Israel Houghton. It's a nice song and has great energy but it's not the song for the hour. Congregations are very critical and discerning. Most times they are judgmental. They have their top ten playlist and anything outside of that is not favored. They can be personality driven. If it's not a certain person leading, then they don't want to engage. I think that's a culture and practice that needs to be broken in the body of Christ. It hinders God.

Corporate worship or congregational worship is not just about the people being ministered to, it's also about the minister's being ministered to. In a corporate setting everyone is actively or should be actively participating and seeking the presence of God. Leaders have a responsibility and congregations have a responsibility. I will discuss further in the next chapter.

Use the written, infallible word worship leaders! It's acceptable to sing God's word. Think about it. God is obligated to respond to His word. It activates heaven on your behalf. Think about the power of corporate worship and everyone singing in unity the truth of scripture. That image is powerful and definitely effective. It is a sure way to experience a new level of demonstration of glory.

Everything you do should be founded upon love. Love is a firm foundation in which we build our lives on. God loved us so much that he sent His only begotten Son to die for us. Every worship leader should recognize that love is the key ingredient when leading a congregation. God's perfect love casts out all fear and is literally violent for us, His creation. Practice love and perfect it so that you lead out of a compassionate heart not with an attitude of judgement. Lead with love and mercy. It is a sure reflection of the Father. When you see that the congregation is not ready, ask the Holy Spirit how to proceed.

As a worship leader I am a representative of the *King of Kings*. I'm a Levite. I should be stamped by heaven. When I make prophetic gestures, decrees, or flow prophetically it should always come from the Father. It sometimes means you are a pioneer. You are on the front lines. You are leading the way. Pray and ask for strategy. Intercede for the congregation to desire a closer relationship with Christ that compels them to worship Him out of their pure love and reverence for Him. You can then learn to not respond out of your flesh on the platform but begin to respond to the darkness. Respond to the forces that have the people chained down forcing them to not be free worshipers. We forget the power and authority we have been given by Christ Jesus. Only the Holy Spirit can break a stony heart and make it a heart of flesh. Have patience with the congregation and know that we wrestle not against flesh and blood but against principalities and don't back down from the opposition, instead ask God to send angels and heavenly reinforcement to assist you in worship.

I have learned in my time of development how to not allow the response of the congregation affect my worship and my ministering. I used to be a wild, loose, cannon. Rebuking from the pulpit and commanding the audience to coerce their worship. Playing the game Simon Says and ministering out of the reserve will definitely have you operating out of a heavy place. But thank God for strong leaders! I do not have weak leaders or weak mentorship. They were wise and bold enough to train me on how to create an atmosphere of freedom. The more I took my eye off the audience's response and their emotional expression and placed my attention and focus on the Father and His beauty, heaven would respond. The presence of God will fill a room and people will naturally respond to the King of Kings. The evil forces will have no other choice but to leave. That is why we need the anointing. Cry out for the anointing! Desire the anointing! Seek the anointing and it shall be found of you! The Word of God says in Isaiah 10:27 NKJV, "It shall come to pass in that day That his burden will be taken away from your shoulder, And his yoke from your neck, And the yoke will be destroyed because of the anointing oil." The anointing destroys the yoke of bondage and removes the burden.

Wisdom for Corporate Worship

- Remember that God initiates, and we respond.
- Make every gathering corporate don't leave the congregation behind.
- Exhortation should be taught and demonstrated before the congregation should be asked to do it.
- Provide scriptures to lay a foundation for songs.
- Encourage participation. Let the anointing and the atmosphere demand the proper response. Do not force a response or punish a congregation for lack of response.
- Keep the focus on exalting Jesus and who He is. Limit songs and exhortation about us and our issues. We don't want to dwell on our condition, but the focus should be on what we can achieve with Christ. Keep the attention on that.
- There will be tough atmospheres. Rely on the Holy Spirit to see what the need is in the atmosphere.
- Always have a call to worship.
- Be spontaneous and flexible. Leave room for the unhindered flow of the Holy Spirit.
- Make time for Lament in worship just as the Psalmist, always resolve it in the hope and promises of Jesus Christ. Acknowledge it but don't stay there.
- Don't expect something from them that you yourself are not willing to give. If you want vulnerability in the response you have to display vulnerability in your worship.

Leading a Team

When leading a team remember these two words…love and grace. Embrace the grace that God has measured unto you for the task He has chosen for you and allow the assignment to transform you as you transform others. I have learned that my love walk is the first thing that needed to be perfected when I began to lead a team. I never had the ability to see what Pastors and other leaders had to experience until I was drafted for the assignment. It will grow you, if you allow it. You become a part of the people business. People need love. People need grace. Remaining teachable is not just for learning the newest songs and the newest books to read and gain more knowledge. Remaining teachable is posturing yourself for correction and rebuke while learning how to provide it for your team. Guard yourself against the spirit of offense and strive to be a healthy leader. This is a process, so again receive the grace. There is a book I recommend called *The Emotionally Healthy Leader* by Peter Scazzero. It will truly teach you about leading from a place of wholeness. I'm learning it makes all the difference.

Worship leaders keep love as your motivator and allow God to bring it forth through you like never before. We are to love people and treat them like Christ. Serve your team and minister to their needs. You will need to be positioned to walk through life with them and if you are weak in your love walk, this will be a challenge.

1 Corinthians 13:1-3 NLT says, "If I could speak all the languages of earth and of angels, but didn't love others, I would only be a noisy gong or a clanging cymbal. If I had the gift of prophecy, and if I understood all of

God's secret plans and possessed all knowledge, and if I had such faith that I could move mountains, but didn't love others, I would be nothing. If I gave everything to the poor and even sacrificed my body, I could boast about it; but if I didn't love others, I would have gained nothing. "

Many leaders cannot lead because they have not made the switch in their minds to a place of leadership. I was there. I did it. I had to fight to transition and it almost cost me my promotion in God. God cannot use you if you're straddling between two seasons. He needs you to fully embrace in your mind that you have received the promotion. For example, imagine you just moved from a picker at a warehouse to a top managerial position. You are now required to go to meetings and create schedules and do employee evaluations. That is so awesome, right? Now picture your salary has changed, you used to work on the floor and now you have your own office with an office phone, they even gave you a name tag. You come to work and still hop on the machine and grab the spreadsheet to pick. Everything has changed, but in your mind you are still a picker on the main floor working. It is the same with leadership. As leaders, we must transition in our minds and hearts and embrace what the new is so that we can begin to see it flourish.

As a worship leader you should be constantly training and cultivating your team. Get creative and ask their opinions on what they desire to know, or what they struggle with in the music ministry and then *TRAIN*. Remember Joshua was being cultivated and groomed as he served Moses so when the time came God saw him fit to lead. If the worship ministry cannot continue on without you, I would say you are not a very good steward over the assignment. However, do not be condemned! If you are in a ministry that just does not have the participation in the music ministry, then cultivate what is on the inside of you and pray for God to send capable and willing vessels to connect. Continue to give your best! God will get the glory!

The first duty of the worship leader concerns the administration of church worship. This involves planning, organizing, and superintending the worship liturgy. Whether or not one adopts Webbers, diagram of preparation, worship, and response, the worship leader must develop a form that provides the framework for the meeting between God and His people. Next, the worship leader is responsible for instructing the congregation in worship, especially the form of worship characteristic of the church's worship tradition or denominational affiliation. In addition, this worship instruction should include teaching on the history, theory, and practice of worship in the Christian church generally. Finally, the training of lay worship leaders by the elder-bishop (leader, overseer) ensures the continuity of the worship tradition and congregational participation. With that being said, as worship leaders you are to be developing and cultivating worship in your contexts so that the presence of God can be experienced in worship every time you minister.

If you feel that after reading these duties that you are not fulfilling the totality of your role then here's what you do.

Action Steps to Take

1. Evaluate your music ministry.
2. Assess your team for areas of strength and areas of opportunity.
3. Assess your heart.
4. Seek God in prayer and ask for divine strategy and vision on how He would like to see the worship develop in the ministry.
5. Schedule a meeting with your superior. It can be the Worship Pastor, Senior Leadership, or both, and get their feedback and wisdom.
6. Then start by incorporating small changes to foster an environment of worship and prayer. This would be a great way to start to engage your team with gatherings for worship and prayer, teachings on worship and worship ministry, providing demonstration and sharing vision so that your team can have a sense of direction.

4

The Worship Congregant

We have a responsibility when we come together corporately to collectively invite the work and flow of the Holy Spirit. There is power in corporate worship. Hebrews 10:25 NKJV says, *"not forsaking the assembling of ourselves together, as is the manner of some, but exhorting one another, and so much the more as you see the Day approaching."* When we gather on one accord, the Holy Spirit is able to work in the lives of the people. In Nehemiah 8 and 9, we see Ezra the priest leading the people in corporate worship.

"...Ezra brought the Book of the Law before the assembly, which included men and women and all the children old enough to understand ... All the people listened closely to the Book of the Law."
Nehemiah 8:2-3 NLT

"Then Ezra praised the Lord, the great God, and all the people chanted, 'Amen! Amen!' as they lifted their hands. Then they bowed down and worshiped the Lord with their faces to the ground."
Nehemiah 8:6 NLT

"On October 31 the people assembled again, and this time they fasted and dressed in burlap and sprinkled dust on their heads. Those of Israelite descent separated themselves from all foreigners as they confessed their own sins and the sins of their ancestors. They remained standing in place for three hours while the Book of the Law of the Lord their God was read aloud to them. Then for three more hours they confessed their sins and worshiped the Lord their God."
Nehemiah 9:1-5 NLT

In Nehemiah, we see the people of God gathered together to hear the word of the Lord proclaimed, and to worship. After the Word of God was proclaimed, they confessed their sins and worshiped for 3 hours. Can you imagine a church service likened to that today? Most believers complain if a service extends past an hour or two. Imagine 6 hours of corporate worship. I don't want to get caught up in the time spent, but there is something to be said concerning what we value and treasure. Are we hungry for God and open to what He wants to accomplish on the earth? Do we desire to know Him intimately and be in His presence?

What's powerful about this passage of scripture is that the Children of Israel gathered together, heard the word of the Lord, worshiped together, and then dedicated their lives and made vows to the Lord. But even more importantly, this corporate assembly was generational. In Nehemiah 8:2, it stated that the children (as young as could understand) gathered with the assembly. We see a generation of young people learning what worship is at an early age. From the young to the old, the people of God were taught what it means to worship the Lord and witness the power of corporate worship to the Lord.

Have you ever visited a church and you were excited to hear the preacher preach because your friend has been raving about his teachings? You have watched sermon videos and you know that God is going to speak to you in the service. You get dressed and head to the service. When you arrive, you are welcomed by smiling greeters and seated by an amazing usher. You can tell you're in a beautiful house of worship. You observe the members greeting one another and catching each other up from their week. The service countdown begins, and everyone gets in position to start service. Then the worship leader opens up the service with a call to worship that includes a scripture and prayer. You see the smiling praise team members faces. They are excited to minister. They are energized. They open up with the first song of the set list and you sing along and lift your hands but in your mind, you are thinking, "I wonder what the message will be today!" You have an expectation for God to show up and have His way. Well, you are the Worship Congregant.

A worship congregant is defined as an active participant in corporate worship. Corporate Worship is where people gather to receive from God through worship, word, and fellowship through the work of the Holy Spirit for the edification and building up. Corporate worship is not just music. I repeat, it is not *JUST* the music! Prayer and giving of tithes and offerings are also considered times of worship.

Unlike in the Bible, worship is not taught in the body of Christ like it should be today. Just as there are so many twisted doctrines about Jesus and His ministry there are so many about worship. What is proper? What is considered acceptable worship? What place is best? Many believers and nonbelievers alike have no clue about worship, and pastors are at times at a loss of how to teach this. Many pastors are not worshipers themselves, so it is hard to teach something you yourself have not learned.

Revelation only becomes revelation when it has been lived.

I believe that is why God is raising up pastors of worship and equipping more and more men and women of God in worship to be able to reach back. There are no current teachings on worship being taught by senior pastors. There is no intentional training in most churches concerning worship. Congregations have to be taught what worship is and what worship is not. As a worship congregant you should be aware of the theology of worship that your ministry has. What are their beliefs concerning worship? Why does the ministry do what they do concerning worship or the entire service? For example, why does the ministry start with an upbeat song first and do a slower tempo following. Not all fast songs are praise and not all slow songs are worship. Who made that up? I have no clue, but it is what we follow, and consider it law which is a concern in the Body of Christ. We have moved our focus from what is really important in worship to man-made protocols that do not reach the heart of God.

It is critical to say everything is a performance. The expressions of worship are different but it's the same Holy Ghost. Sometimes He does not come and blow us away because we are so focused on the praise team and the song choice instead of placing your heart on an altar and crying out to God and repenting. Then and only then can He decide to manifest His glory. It's not all on the worship leader or the team. It's a body. It is corporate worship. Local gathering. The church and body of Christ needs training. People don't understand what it takes, and we are quick to say the Glory did not come but did you worship. Did you invite Him? Having a real relationship with God does not equate to glory or anointing being made known in a corporate gathering. God decides that. He's the initiator. If you only have a hunger privately but no expectation corporately, then you cannot expect glitter corporately. He sees the heart. Not just the heart of the leader but the heart of the people. The heart of the corporate body. That is just as important as who is leading is so easy as the participant in worship to become a spectator. You observe and critique, but you do not understand the power of you being disengaged. Now I am not speaking of the unsaved who have not received Jesus Christ as their personal Lord and Savior. I am speaking to the person that is connected to a local church and you know what is acceptable to God, but you choose to still walk in a religious mindset. You desire to be entertained and inspired to praise and worship the God that you proclaim you love and serve wholeheartedly… more than anything. The very thought of Him should be inspiration enough to give Him your best every day of your lives.

Behold, how good and how pleasant it is for brethren to dwell together in unity!
Psalm 133:1 NKJV

Beloved friends, what does all this imply? When you conduct your meetings, you should always let everything be done to build up the church family. Whether you share a song of praise, a teaching, a divine revelation, or a tongue and interpretation, let each one contribute what strengthens others.
1 Corinthians 14:26 TPT

5

The Worship Overseer

This section is designed for the Worship Pastor/Minister of Music/Band Director

RESPONSIBILITY

You have been entrusted with the assignment of Worship Overseer in your local house. Congratulations! Your leadership trusts you and they have a desire to see the worship go to the next level under your leadership as you partner with the Holy Spirit. It may be frightening but I assure you that when you rely on the Holy Spirit you will have all you need. Be intentional to seek God about how you should approach this assignment and give it 100%. This is God's assignment and you are leading God's people so do not take lightly what is before you. Here are some things I would suggest to you as you walk in your grace and embrace the assignment.

- Evaluate your team.
- Get organized.
- Decide who will assist you in this assignment.

- What immediate things need to be implemented, changed, or removed.
- Pray and ask the Holy Spirit for strategy and vision.

VISION

In order to truly have vision for your worship ministry you have to carry the vision of the visionaries. Vision comes from God and the mission comes from man. God will download the vision and insight on what He desires to have accomplished and then you implement mission which is developing a strategy on how to carry it out. As a leader you want to have a clear written vision so that you and your team can know where they are going as you begin to set order, implement and train.

- Have a meeting with Senior Leadership and receive their vision for the music ministry. What would they like to see done? How do they desire for it to evolve? What jurisdiction do you have? This is also the time to share your vision and what you desire to bring to the table. Present your innovative ideas. Do not be afraid of receiving correction and guidance to get to an agreement of ministry.
- Write the vision down and make it plain.
- Discuss with your ministry the direction you desire to go and be transparent about where you see the ministry and according to what you and senior leadership have discussed where it should be going.
- Give short-term goals and long-term goals.
- Do not overwhelm your ministry.
- Roll out small changes or roll out big changes. Rely on leadership and the Holy Spirit to know what should be done first.
- Get feedback.

TRAINING

It is so important to train your ministry. We perish due to a lack of knowledge. Training and equipping produces excellence. Your teams need teachings to grow and progress in worship ministry. Always allow space to ask questions and challenge them in their thinking. You can deal with multiple issues by relying on the Holy Spirit in answering just one question. Bring in trainers as well. Train yourself...Have a good balance when it comes to this. Training ignites passion and hunger and helps your ministry practice. They learn what is acceptable and how they can utilize it when they are ministering.

- Host trainings.
- Start small by debriefing services.
- Give honest and spirit led feedback.
- Challenge by providing scenarios and advising proper responses and engagement.
- Explain why things are the way they are in alignment with the vision.
- All info should align with the vision of ministry and local house.
- Be creative. Do not always make trainings lecture style. People need to be more interactive. There are different learning styles.
- Allow the ministry team to give feedback and express their challenges. These times can bring real freedom and healing.
- As the leader you should always be going through training yourself.

Here are two things that I have observed in worship pastors and ministers of music.

Tradition vs. God

Many times, we come from religious backgrounds. We have grown up in church and started playing on the organ at 9 years old. We know church. Be mindful to not allow your tradition, and how you have always done it, to hinder what God is doing. God is the same and He never changes but many times He does a new thing to ignite a fire and start a revival that His people may be compelled to do greater works. With leading a music ministry, you must begin to sense what season the house is in and what needs to take place within the music ministry, so God can do a new thing. Do not get complacent and stuck in the pattern of, "We always do these songs! It has always been this way!" Yes, you may normally sing a hymn for communion but one particular Sunday, it may need to be a prophetic song about His sacrifice and resurrection. Do not be so traditional that you are no longer open to the instruction of the Lord within an atmosphere. Walking and following God requires constant change. As the ministry evolves the worship should evolve. It should be perfected (mature) for the people. Follow the cloud and the fire, it will lead you to the land flowing with milk and honey!

Lead them without Losing them

Be mindful that although you are a leader you are also a servant. Servanthood is extremely important when it comes to modeling a behavior for your ministry. Always strive for your word to be bond when it comes to them. Being present, starting and ending on time, giving and receiving feedback and dwelling with your music ministry according to knowledge will maintain a level of respect and honor. You want to gain the trust of your teams by knowing what you are talking about and honoring their time and commitment especially when your ministry functions as volunteer basis. Be sure to honor them in word and deed. Be honest about things when they are in error and then always encourage.

Help them without hurting them.

Develop a wisdom to know how to deal with certain issues as they arise. For me, I have to continue to come up with creative ideas and ways to keep my team engaged and excited about God. I cannot afford to become complacent because then complacency flows from the head down. I have learned to handle correction quickly with wisdom and love. Always be the example! In leading a music ministry, I am the leader and the servant. I give of myself and I also set the standards for what should be. What does that mean? I cannot be late to rehearsals and sound checks and expect punctuality from my team. I cannot be disengaged during service and expect my team to walk in readiness. I cannot mandate a dress code for the women and I myself do not honor and value what is expected. I cannot say learn this music and I myself have not learned it. I cannot encourage my team to read scripture and pray outside of Sundays and Wednesdays and I myself do not commune with Jesus. It is hypocritical, and people see through that. There are exceptions to the rule; indeed. However, you should always be on the front line and model the behavior you desire to see.

People watch more than they listen!

Your team should follow you as you follow Christ and expect the fruit of the Holy Spirit to be in you. Know that the simplest things make the difference and you want your ministry to value your pour. As an overseer you should continuously be working on your character and have accountability to keep you grounded and effective.

APPENDIX A
Prayers

PRAYER FOR FAMILY AND GENERATIONS

God of mercy and truth, we honor who You are, and we thank You for Your truth that lasts through the ages. Your commandments and ways go through generations. We thank You for Your truth being instilled into families and that trees of life will spring forth in families. Impart Your wisdom and Your ways into the hearts of parents and guardians so that they will train up Kingdom citizens and they will not depart from it. Allow households to be restored and for godly behavior to be demonstrated in households Father. Break and cancel every generational curse and iniquity that would seek to poison generations and we command heavenly lineages in the earth to be established. Let Your will concerning families be established on the earth as You so desire it in heaven. We pray that Your truth would dismantle lies from the enemy that are sent to destroy families. We praise You for the power You hold that when You speak words they become truth and they remain throughout generations. Oh God of Abraham, Isaac and Jacob we praise You for generational blessings flowing out into the earth and healthy God-fearing and Bible-honoring families. In Jesus name, Amen.

PRAYER FOR THE WORSHIP

Father God, I thank You for the power and purpose of worship. It is amazing to know that worship is for You and for our benefit. I thank You Lord for purifying my worship and showing me how to properly give You worship that is due Your name. Teach me Your ways that I may know what is acceptable and pleasing in Your sight. Let me not be a worshiper in words or outward appearance alone but let my heart be postured to worship You. I reverence You because You are the Almighty God and Creator and You deserve worship and praise. I pray Lord that the world may see worship for what it truly is and what it isn't. I pray we as the body of Christ would devote our lives to worshiping You in Spirit and in Truth as we know that is what the Father looks for. Thank You Jesus for the sacrifice you gave that I may have salvation and a life full of abundance but also that I may be reconciled back to the Father. Because of what You did on the cross I can come boldly before the throne of grace. I have access because You decided to die and rise from the dead. Holy Spirit guide me into all truth and create in me a clean heart and renew a right spirit within me that I will forever give proper and pure praise and worship. I pray Lord that You will find delight in my worship. In the name of Jesus, I pray, Amen.

PRAYER FOR THE WORSHIPER

Thank You Lord for calling me to be a worshiper. Thank You for the understanding and revelation of what that truly means. I pray Lord that as I present my body and life as a living sacrifice that You will be glorified. I appreciate Your written word which is the standard for how I should live. I thank You that Your word provides me with instruction, guidance and wisdom that I may draw closer to You. I thank You Lord that I will keep a fresh desire to worship You daily. I will be unashamed to declare Your great works and praise Your name. I lay aside every weight and let go of every idol that has come between our ever-growing relationship. I trust that through me living a life reflective of worship that I will have a great witness and my light will shine for all to see. I give You praise in advance for the many people that will be drawn to You through my life. I praise You! In Jesus' name I pray. Amen.

PRAYER FOR THE WORSHIP LEADER

Father, I want to say thank You for the beautiful ministry of worship leadership. You have placed so many gifts and talents on the inside of Your children to be effective for Your glory. I thank You Lord for raising up more worship leaders for Your glory. I pray Lord that every worship leader would understand the severity of the mandate You have given and begin to seek You for wisdom and guidance on how to be a worship leader. Thank You Lord for providing a vast amount of resources such as this manual, other books, videos, conferences, schools and local churches that have accepted the mandate to equip and train leaders for Kingdom impact. I am grateful that I get to be a part of Your plan Lord. You have placed a heart of worship inside of me and anointed me with oil. I thank You! I pray Lord that You teach me how to surrender to You daily that I may be used for Your glory. Not just for Sunday but that I may be able to minister daily through my life, my thoughts, and my interactions with others. Lord do not remove Your presence from me for without it I am nothing. I have no other choice but to serve You and give Your name praise. I pray that I will walk in a boldness and with an authority knowing that You will not desert me. Knowing that with You I have everything I need. Teach me how to worship You! I seek Your face for revelation of You in the most intimate way. The deeper I know You the deeper I can worship You. I want to be like the creatures who day and night are lavishing You with worship because they are seeing more of You by the second. Show me the ways you desire to be adored. What pleases You Master? I desire to ascend Your holy hill and give You reverence all the days of my life. Father help me to desire sonship more than I desire service. Let me desire fellowship with You more than I desire to sing and lift my voice. I want to find my refuge and my rest in You always. I thank You for victory over my mind and over my body that I be purified for You to be used. I rejoice because I know that as I take care of Your matters, You are working on behalf of mine. I love You and I adore Your Holy name that is above every name Jesus, Amen.

PRAYER FOR THE WORSHIP CONGREGANT

I recognize that I have a responsibility to participate in corporate worship as a worshiper. I thank You Lord for the revelation of the power of the gathering. Allow me to always maintain my focus and my adoration for You always. No matter where I am. Let it not be for show but let what I encounter at home spillover publicly. I want to see Your glory like never before. I want to see the things that I read about come to life before my very eyes Lord. Father help me to not take Your holy presence for granted. I pray against the spirit of complacency and resistance in the name of Jesus. Let there be a free flow Holy One. Let there be a habitation for Your holy presence a dwelling place; a tabernacle that You find delight in. I thank You Lord that when we gather there will be an expectation and pull for Your glory. If You don't show up Lord, then what do we have…Nothing! Let us not look to man or woman to be our priest but let us look to the High Priest for access to the throne room of heaven. I thank You Lord for miracles, signs and wonders breaking out in churches all over the world. Revival happening in regions and victory ringing in the camp because the unity of the brethren has showed up. I bless You and I thank You for what You designed unity and prayer to accomplish. In Jesus' name, Amen.

PRAYER FOR THE WORSHIP OVERSEER

Lord, for every task set before me I say I accept with a secure yes. I am secure in You holding me. Give me insight for every stage of the ministry. Show me how to handle situations and how to lead the people You have entrusted in my care. Show me how to be truly effective and how to train up others that they may be secure and embrace what You have called for them to do in the earth for the kingdom of heaven. I thank You Lord for innovative ways to connect with those under my leadership and the wisdom to meet every need according to Your will. I come against every spirit that would seek to bring division, strife, backbiting, jealousy, comparison, rebellion, pride and fear. I break it in Jesus name! Allow my people to be covered and protected by angels that they be untouched by the formed weapons. For every leader and shepherd, I pray Father God in the name of Jesus that You would cover them in Your blood. I thank You for the delicate task of leading people for Your glory, but Lord I thank You for keeping each overseer covered in glory. Let them lead out of a healthy place. A place full of integrity and love for the sheep. I pray for divine insight for every overseer. In Jesus' Name, Amen.

PRAYER FOR RESTORATION OF THE WILDERNESS WORSHIP LEADER

Lord I recognize that I have been operating out of a place of hurt and offense with my giftings and callings. I allowed the negative and positive experiences I had to turn me away from Your church, Your body, and You. I repent for this now. I ask for Your forgiveness and I now understand the error in which I have operated in. Wash me of all unrighteousness and heal me in those broken places that have been wounded and motivated me to leave Your order. I thank You Lord for granting me access to forgiveness and the Father. Now Lord, I activate Jeremiah 3:11-15 in my life. I ask You Lord for wisdom in selecting a covering, leadership. Show me who to connect with. Show me who can embrace me and lead me and nurse me back to health. I need Your guidance. Until You lead me to that place, I submit my gifts and callings to You and I make a commitment to come under Your covering. I will not operate without Your leading and Your approval. I humble myself that Your mighty hand may be at work in my life. I'm sorry Lord and I thank You for granting me mercy and showing me Your unfailing love. I trust You! In Jesus Name, Amen.

PRAYER FOR THE PURE IN HEART WORSHIPER

For I have tasted and seen of the goodness of You Lord. I love everything You are, and I thank You for being my God. I thank You for the purpose of worship and for revealing Your heart to me. I pray Father that I will forever have a pure heart before You. Continue to create in me a clean heart and renew a right spirit within me that I may forever please You and honor You with my life and my worship before You. I just want to please You. I pray that every weapon formed against me to deter me and distract me not prosper according to Your word so that I may walk in victory. I thank You Lord for enabling me to maintain a pure heart before You. That is what I desire Lord. May I forever glorify Your name no matter what I experience or come up against all the glory belongs to You. In Jesus Name, Amen.

PRAYER FOR THE RELIGIOUS WORSHIPER

Father forgive me for the spirit of religion that I have operated in. I recognize that I am religious, and I desire to be changed. I know You desire relationship and not religion. You hate religion. I want to hate what You hate and love what You love. I desire to be set free from this spirit that has been wrapped around my neck suffocating me from the true authentic relationship You desire with me. I pray for Your forgiveness. I ask that the blood of Jesus cleanses me from anything not like You that would hinder me or block me from getting closer to You. I close all doors and I surrender to the work of the Holy Spirit in my life. Help me Holy Spirit to understand the heart of God. Teach me how to truly worship God not with my lips or on Sundays but with my life, with my heart. I want to encounter the fullness of what You have to offer. I no longer wish to be bound to tradition and pass down rites of passage that hold no power and don't display love. I want who You are. I want to know what is acceptable and pleasing to You. I receive You now. I believe that You are stepping in now to help me and bring answers and restore relationship. I welcome You Holy God. Take me deeper until I know the complete expression of Your love and power. In Jesus Name, Amen.

PRAYER FOR SPEAKING IN TONGUES

Heavenly Father, I come in the name of Jesus Christ and I desire the baptism of the Holy Spirit with the evidence of speaking in tongues. Please forgive me for my sins and any unforgiveness I may have, I release it right now in Jesus' name. Your word says that the gift of the Holy Spirit comforts us and guides us. He also gives us access to other gifts of the Spirit and we have access to God's power to walk out the assignment and mandate on our life. I want that kind of power to do Your will Lord. I know that the receiving of this gift is supernatural and a miracle because it surpasses all human reasoning. Your word says that I can have it and I receive this gift by faith in the name of Jesus. Baptize me with Your fire! I know my life will never be the same. I thank you for Your baptism and help me to continue living for You. May this fire never burn out and always keep me close to You. I love you Lord and thank You for this new heavenly language and for the gift of the Holy Spirit. In Jesus' name, Amen.

APPENDIX B

EXERCISES FOR YOU, YOUR TEAM, AND YOUR CONGREGATION

(After information comes Activation)

FAITH EXERCISES

Faith Exercise 1:

Jot down some scriptures on faith and boldness. Declare them over yourself daily. I listed a few but there are several.

Mark 9: 23-24

Jesus said to him, "If you can believe, all things are possible to him who believes." Immediately the father of child cried out and said with tears, "Lord I believe; help my unbelief!"

Philippians 4:13

I can do all things through Christ who strengthens me.

2 Timothy 1:7

For God has not given us a spirit of fear, but of power and of love and of a sound mind.

Luke 10:19

Behold, I give you the authority to trample on serpents and scorpions, and over all the power of the enemy, and nothing by any means shall hurt you.

Romans 10:17

So, then faith comes by hearing, and hearing by the word of God.

Faith Exercise 2:

Pray for faith to be given unto you. We all have a measure of faith.

Faith Exercise 3:

Engage the Holy Spirit in small things to develop confidence and assurance of hearing the voice of God. Find out how he speaks to you and look for that every time.

(Ex. Holy Spirit where are my keys? What should I wear today? What emotion am I feeling? What do you think about this specific situation?)

Faith Exercise 4:

When leading ask the Holy Spirit to sing through you and yield by trusting and obeying. Begin to sing in the spirit or act out what you heard and or saw Him say.

PRACTICE EXERCISES

Practice Exercise 1:

Journaling is great. Begin to write down songs and lyrics that the Holy Spirit gives to you.

Practice Exercise 2:

Sing scripture. Go to a Psalm or a chapter in Isaiah and sing the verses. This is great practice. Place a melody to the words you read.

Practice Exercise 3:

Stir yourself up by praying in the Holy Spirit and then sing what you feel God is saying. Record it and playback. Have someone in authority judge it.

Practice Exercise 4:

One sure way to get comfortable prophetically flowing is by keeping yourself stirred. You should frequently sing in the spirit. Just as you sing in the natural, sing in the spirit. Then ask the Holy Spirit to reveal what you just sang. Write it down.

Practice Exercise 5:

Experiment flowing and creating a spontaneous flow. A spontaneous flow goes hand in hand with creativity. Take a familiar song and change up the melody or the rhythm. Repeat a phrase multiple time. Record it and listen back. Try going from one song to another song while keeping the same theme.

(Ex. There is none like you Marvin Sapp transitioning to Nobody Greater by Vashawn Mitchell

(Ex. Praise God from whom all blessings flow transitioning into We Exalt Thee)

HUNGER EXERCISES

Hunger Exercise: 1

Find like-minded worshipers like you and build relationship. Worship leaders should have a community who uplifts, encourages, and supports, and introduces you to new things.

Hunger Exercise 2:

Attend a worship conference or training. There are multiple workshops and resources available to you. Be selective in choice. There is something for every aspect regarding worship. Don't be afraid to travel. If you are located in a region that does not have any sound teaching or training available, be willing to invest in your development.

Hunger Exercise 3:

Read books and watch video content.

GROUP ACTIVITIES

Group Activity 1:

Host a Glory Party where you gather with people to soak in His presence. Make it BYOB (bring your own Bible). Pray and worship and then allow the Holy Spirit to birth out new songs and ideas from that time. Record everything so you are still engaged with the setting. This can be done on a personal level with a community of believers or with a team/ music ministry.

Group Activity 2:

Schedule a band retreat/clinic where the musicians can experience a time of refreshing and filling. They also assist in carrying the sound and need to be considered as well.

Group Activity 3:

Have your music ministry gather for times of intercession. Be strategic! Every rehearsal should not be music it needs to meet the current needs of the music ministry. Complete a training on intercession and praise and have them demonstrate.

Group Activity 4:

When introducing a new song, explain the purpose of the song and scripture reference. Ask your team questions like, "Why is this relevant? What is the revelation behind it? Allow them to discuss.

Group Activity 5:

Always work on connecting within your ministry. Find out about people's lives and what struggles they have. Incorporate times of discipleship. Care about the person and not just their gift.

Group Activity 6:

Plan times of fellowship where the music ministry can bond as brothers and sisters in Christ. It helps build unity and trust within a team. You are willing to follow people you know.

APPENDIX C

GLOSSARY OF TERMS

Frequently Used Terms
Glossary

Adversary: Satan, the devil

> *Be sober, be vigilant; because your adversary the devil walks about like a roaring lion, seeking whom he may devour. - 1 Peter 5:8 NKJV*

Baptism of the Holy Spirit with the evidence of speaking in tongues:

> *For John baptized you in water, but in a few days from now you will be baptized in the Holy Spirit. - Acts 1:5 (Additional scripture references: Acts 2:1-47 TPT)*

> *And when Paul laid his hands on each of the twelve, the Holy Spirit manifested and they immediately spoke in tongues and prophesied. - Acts 19:6-7 TPT*

Consecration: the sacred act of dedicating something to God, sanctifying it, and making it holy, commonly your mind and body

> *And do, dear brothers and sisters, I plead with you to give your bodies to God, because of all he has done for you. Let them be a living and holy sacrifice- the kind he will find acceptable....-Romans 12:1 NLT*

Faith: Complete confidence or trust in someone or something

> *Now faith brings our hopes into reality and becomes the foundation needed to acquire the things we long for. It is all the evidence required to prove what is still unseen.*
> *Hebrews 11:1 TPT*

Fasting: to abstain from anything for a spiritual purpose.

From the moment of his baptism, Jesus was overflowing with the Holy Spirit. He was taken by the Spirit from the Jordan into the lonely wilderness of Judea to experience the ordeal of testing by the accuser for forty days. He ate no food during this time and ended his forty-day fast hungry. It was then the devil said to him, "If you are really the Son of God, command this stone to turn into a loaf of bread for you." Jesus replied, "I will not! For it is written in the Scriptures, 'Life does not come only from eating bread but from God. Life flows from every revelation from his mouth,'"
-Luke 4:2-4 TPT

All that time I had eaten no rich food. No meat or wine crossed my lips, and I used no fragrant lotions until those three weeks had passed. -Daniel 10: 3 NLT

Fear: an unpleasant often strong emotion caused by anticipation or awareness of danger (Merriam-Webster)

Glory: the manifested presence of God.

For the very glory you have given to me I have given them so that they will be joined together as one and experience the same unity that we enjoy. -John 17:22 TPT

Holy Spirit: a person of the Trinity. Spirit of truth. Jesus's Spirit that dwells on the inside of the believer. Known as the Comforter and a Guide. He leads us into all truth.

Intercession or Intercede: praying on behalf of another, to stand in the gap.

I looked for someone among them who would build up the wall and stand before me in the gap on behalf of the land so I would not have to destroy it, but I found no one. - Ezekiel 22:30 NIV

Spirit of Fear: a weapon against the believer from Satan. The opposite of faith in operation designed to dismantle and hinder the believer.

> *For God has not given us a spirit of fear, but of power and of love and of a sound mind. - II Timothy 1:7 NKJV*

Spiritual realm: a spiritual kingdom where spiritual matters dwell & take place.

Warfare or Spiritual Warfare: fighting against the work of the enemy (Satan).

> *For our struggle is not against flesh and blood, but against the rulers, against the authorities, against the powers of this dark world and against the spiritual forces of evil in the heavenly realms. - Ephesians 6:12 NIV*

> *Praise be to the Lord my Rock, who trains my hands for war, my fingers for battle. - Psalm 144:1 NIV*

Vagabond: Wanderer from the Hebrew word, *nuwa*, meaning to wander up and down, to cause to wander.

ABOUT THE AUTHOR

Sarenina Y. Bonner is both a skilled and anointed vocalist. Music is her passion and worship her heart. Having served in music ministry from the age of 13, she has learned the importance of cultivating a lifestyle of worship off the platform to have a greater impact on the platform in order for God to be glorified. She believes that cultivating your gifts for Kingdom use is vital to operating in the fullness of God for His glory and the edification of His people.

A native of Memphis, TN, Sarenina earned her Bachelor of Arts in Music Vocal Performance from Fisk University. During her college years, she served as a soloist and member of the world-renowned Fisk Jubilee Singers© under the direction of Dr. Paul Kwami.

Sarenina specializes in proper technique, vocal health, and all aspects of performance. She was an itinerant vocalist in Nashville, performing at various churches and musical events. She has also participated in multiple ensembles throughout her 10+ year career.

Additional accomplishments include travel to numerous cities in the U.S. and England performing Negro spirituals, art songs, gospel and performing in concerts with great artists such as Keb Mo, Wynonna Judd, Michael McDonald, Everett Miller, and Micah Stampley. She was also a background vocalist for Micah Stampley in concert and Everett Miller which aired on Bobby Jones Gospel taped in Nashville, TN.

Currently grooming new and upcoming vocalists and worship leaders, Sarenina recognizes the value in training and pouring out what God has given to her. This ministry was birthed through the Holy Spirit's leading to supply a need for ministries and leaders who are seeking to grow in worship knowledge and strengthen their teams.

Sarenina Y. Bonner is the Assistant Professor of Modern Music, Vocals at Visible Music College, Memphis campus. She also actively serves as Worship Leader of Divine Life Church under the leadership of Apostle Tony & Pastor Felecia Wade.

CPSIA information can be obtained
at www.ICGtesting.com
Printed in the USA
LVHW092107040619
620129LV00005B/5/P